REFLECTIONS ON SCIENCE AND POETRY

HITOSHI OSHIMA

花　書房
図書出版

JN062808

Published by Hana Shoin Publishing 2022

Copyright © Hitoshi Oshima 2022

All the illustrations including the one on the cover of this book are created by Tana Oshima.

ISBN 978-4-86561-268-4

Hana-Shoin Publishing, Shirokane 2-9-6, Chuo-ku, Fukuoka, Japan 810-0012
https://www.kijima-p.co.jp/business-guide/hanashoin/

Printed by Kijima Printing, Inc., Shirokane 2-9-6, Chuo-ku, Fukuoka, Japan 810-0012

Reflections on Science and Poetry

Born in Kamakura, Japan, in 1948, Hitoshi Oshima is a Professor Emeritus in Fukuoka University, Japan, specializing in comparative literature. His recent research interest is in the modern efforts of bridging science and poetry. A former president of JCLA(2011-15) and member of the Executive Council of ICLA (2013-19), he published *El pensamiento japonés* (Edición Universitaria de Buenos Aires, 1987), *Le Développement d'une Pensée Mythique -pour comprendre la pensée japonaise-* (Editions Osiris, Paris, 1994) and others.

Mathematical Science and Poetry

Foreword

This book is composed of five articles the common theme of which is "science and poetry". The theme is extremely important because we are living in the age of science and the problem of the "two cultures" has not been solved yet. Those who study science know little of poetry; those who consider themselves literary know hardly anything of science; and philosophers who are supposed to make a bridge between them take neither science nor poetry seriously enough. The scary situation continues.

The author of the book hopes to contribute to the lessening of the ditch that has separated science and poetry for such a long time. He believes that there is a connecting point of the two, for they are both products of the same human brain.

The problem of the ditch between science and poetry is not new. Toward the end of the 19th century, some Western intellectuals already wrote on it questioning the premises of modern science that had left common sense and poetry behind. Henri Bergson manifested his fear about modern science for its tendency to quantify the unquantifiable: in his *Essai sur les données immediates de la conscience* (1889), he condemned those who treated time as a measurable object.

As for scientists, Henri Poincaré who founded topological mathematics tried to give equal values to poetry and science wishing to make up a harmonious view on the two (*Savants et écrivains*, 1910). Gaston Bachelard, an epistemologist, also tried to find out their connecting point.

However, despite those efforts, the separation of the two became more and more insurmountable, and finally, we saw C. P. Snow's "The Two Cultures and Scientific Revolution"(1959) appearing as an alert.

Snow's essay impacted the intellectuals all over the world because it was published in the period in which people still had fresh memories of World War II, especially of the A-bombs on Hiroshima and Nagasaki. In the essay, the English physicist-novelist insisted that we should put end to the separation of the two cultures, scientific and humanistic ones. However, despite the impact of the essay, the situation has not changed, the reason of which is obvious. What he proposed concerned the change of the whole system of education which is intimately connected to the whole politico-economical system. As we are living in the world of money and power, not of culture, I am afraid to say that we can hardly hope anything.

This book presents a collection of the past but brilliant challenges against the devastating situation. The first two chapters present two French thinkers of the 20th century: Simone Weil and Claude Lévi-Strauss, who both developed a critical view on modern science in defense of poetry. The third and the fourth chapters present two modern Japanese poetic scientists: Torahiko Terada and Kiyoshi Oka, both of whom developed quite interesting ideas to bridge the "two cultures" mentioned above. The last chapter presents another trial of bridging the two cultures carried on by Kenji Miyazawa, a Japanese mystic who intended to make a fusion of science, religion and poetry. With all these, the author of the book wishes the reader to make due reflections on science and poetry.

Karatsu, Japan
June 2022
Hitoshi Oshma

Contents:

Note: All the translations from French or Japanese into English in this book are mine.

Contents

Chapter 1

Algebra and Poetry in Simone Weil

1

If I am to summarize what Simone Weil was, I would say "a passionate defender of poetry against algebra". Being a teacher of philosophy at lycées, she worked in automobile factories and saw alienation in the workers, from which she concluded that they were lacking in poetry.

> People need poetry like bread. Not poetry enclosed in words that cannot be of any use to them. They need the substance of their everyday life to be poetry. (Condition première d'un travail non servile, 1941) (Weil 1, 219)

As the quotation shows, what she meant by "poetry" was not a literary genre, but that creativity which gives meaning to life.

As for "algebra", she thought of it as a vice, a modern vice, which is shown by the following words in *La pensanteur et la grâce* (*Gravity and Grace*, 1941):

> Money, machinism, algebra. Three monsters of our civilization. Perfect analogy. (Weil 2, 173)

"Money" "machinism" and "algebra", those "three monsters" are in "perfect analogy", she said. She saw them intimately connected to one another.

By "algebra", she meant computation, formalism, unreality, efficiency, convenience, the detail of which we will see later. She saw modern civilization running after money, dependent on algebra alone, in order to realize the most efficient productions by machines.

To her, algebra and poetry were thus opposite to each other. She wished the former not to devastate the latter because she saw the former almost omnipotent over the world. The situation has not changed since then. We are still living in such a world. Thence, Weil is worth knowing.

2

Simone Weil (1909-43) became known to the world by the personal notes she had written before her death in 1943. Gustave Thibon, a friend of hers, found them, edited them to make a book that was published in 1947 with the title *La pensanteur et la grâce* (*Gravity and Grace*). This book full of philosophical insights and mystic view on the universe fascinated postwar readers thirsty of spirituality; they must have found what they needed in there.

Other writings of hers were published later. In 1988, even her *Complete Works* were published. There are more and more readers of her writings, more and more researchers on her.

Perhaps the best book of hers is above mentioned *La pensanteur et la grâce*, which has led people to consider her as a religious thinker. However, we cannot overlook the fact that she was an activist in socio-political movements as well as a persistent critic of modern civilization, especially of science. It is this last aspect of hers which is often neglected that I would like to focus on.

Science was actually her favorite matter in her philosophical reflections. She centered her attention on the development of modern science. As a teacher of philosophy at lycées, she taught history of science more than anything else.

Criticism of modern science, reflection on the workers' physical and mental condition and the war against totalitarianism were what she did apart from reflection on religion. They were all important to her and based on the same spirit which consisted in defense of "poetry" against "algebra".

According to her, modern science was no more science because of its becoming algebraic. Algebra, the origin of which was in Islamic civilization, certainly transformed Greek science based on perception into an abstract system. Thanks to this, modern science could go beyond perception, beyond our reality, to reach the tiniest imaginary world of elementary particles as well as the imaginary end of the universe. But to Weil, the algebraization of science was a catastrophe because it meant not only abandon of reality but also abandon of pursuit of truth. To her, science had to consist in inquiry of truth.

What she called "machinism" as one of the monsters of our time is what we would call "mechanistic world vision". Modern science developed it because of its mathematization of the universe, in other words, digitalization or algebraization. In our modernized societies influenced by it, the production system became mechanistic, the labor system as well. This surely favored the development of capitalism, making some nations prosperous and dominant over others, destroying the traditional community life that was full of "poetry".

It is Karl Marx (1818-83) who made a sharp analysis of the alienation produced by industrialization and propelled by capitalism. Influenced by him or not, Weil saw the same phenomenon in society, and differently from Marx, associated it to the algebraization of science.

3

We know she had some sympathy with Marx at least for a moment, but she did not agree with him as to the solution of the labor problem. "Proletarian revolution" he aimed at was not a good solution at all in her view because she found the recovery of "poetry" much more important for workers than the improvement of their material or social conditions. In abovementioned *La pesanteur et la grâce*, she said:

> Workers need poetry more than bread. They need their life to be poetry, light of eternity. Only religion can be the source of the poetry they need. The opium for people is not religion but revolution. If they are demoralized in a way or another, it is because they are deprived of poetry. (Weil 2, 204)

Her words "The opium for people is not religion but revolution" clearly shows her refusal of Marxism according to which religion was the opium for people.

Weil saw factory workers drunken with Marxist ideology and the dream of proletarian paradise; she saw leftwing militants in Spanish Civil War with a similar ideology that made them blind. She knew that "proletarian revolution" could engender political oppression even worse than the capitalistic one, which was the case with Stalin. She told this vision of hers overtly to Leon Trotsky (1879-1940) whom she met in Paris in 1933. Needless to say, the Russian communist who dreamed of "permanent revolution" did not accept her view.

She differed from Marx just because she thought of work in terms of "poetry". To her, work was a spiritual value, not an economic one. Let us remember what she said on it: "Workers need their life to be poetry, light of eternity." Poetry was a gateway to "eternity" to her.

She also said "Only religion can be the source of the poetry the workers need." Work, poetry, religion, were intimately linked to one another in her view. Work had to be creative, therefore poetical; creation was divine; work as poetry had thence to be reproduction of the divine creation.

This particular view on work and poetry tightly linked to religious insight reminds us of Teresa de Ávila (1515-82). Hannah Murray already pointed it out in her *Poetics of Labor, Simone Weil, St. Teresa and Mysticism* (2016). It seems that Weil never read the Spanish saint's writings.

We know that Weil was born as a Jew in France, a Catholic country, and that Teresa was also born as a Jew and was converted to Catholicism under the pressure of the notorious Inquisition. Having found the spiritual kinship with the latter, Weil could have accepted her Jewish origin more easily. For one of her problems was her constant negation of her cultural origin as Robert Coles, the author of *Simone Weil, a modern pilgrimage* (2001), pointed out.

Weil was an engaged philosopher; she actively participated in socio-political movements till the end of her life. This means she always held a critical attitude as to the reality that surrounded her. If she persistently developed criticism on modern science, it was for the same reason. She thought that modern scientific progress was doing wrong to society because of its mechanistic vision and utilitarianism developed by algebraization of science.

We saw that she lamented the lack of poetry in factory workers' life and that poetry meant life, creativity and gateway to religion. However, we should not overlook the fact that she was a philosopher, which means that poetry was not only the gateway to religion but also to philosophy. And philosophy, she learned it from Alain who was her teacher at Lycée Henri IV. The following is Allain's words that show his philosophical position:

> To think means to say no. Let us remark that yes is a sign of a sleeping man. An awaken man shakes the head and says no. No to what? To the world, to the tyrant, to the preacher? That is just appearance. In all those cases, it is thought that says no to itself. (*Propos sur la religion*, 1938) (Alain, 170)

To say "no" does not simply mean to disagree with others; it means to doubt your belief, your conviction, even your thought. To think means not to stop one's mental activities. What Weil saw in the workers she met in factories was total subjugation to the mechanical system of work, which produced total negation of free mental activities. It is the negation of thinking that she called "lack of poetry". Poetry was the source of thought.

Weil criticized algebraic science because she saw "algebra" as a big cause of the halt of thinking. She saw the civilization of her time in danger because it was dominated by algebraic systems that stopped people's free thinking. In 1942, she left France for New York with her parents to be free from the danger of Nazism, but immediately after her arrival there, she left for London to participate in *La France Libre* organized by General De Gaule. She continued thus her war against Nazism and it was above all to save free thinking from totalitarianism. Her enemy was not Germany nor the Germans but totalitarianism that was depriving people of poetry and free thinking.

3

It is not useless to add here that her brother André (1906-98), a world-famous mathematician, had a critical spirit comparable to hers. Because of his specialty that was algebraic geometry, some could imagine that his sister's criticism of algebra was a kind of reaction against him, which is little probable. We find much in common between their thoughts.

Although they were different in nature, André was "subversive" like Simone. The first university he worked at as a professor was an Indian one, which was already an extraordinary choice. Why did he decide to go there? Because he had great interest in Hinduism, especially in the religious philosophy of *Bhagavad Gita* that he had read in Sanskrit at the age of 16. In his *Souvenirs d'apprentissage* (1991), he confessed that the only form of religion that could satisfy his spirit was in there.

As a mathematician, André is known to have proposed "Weil conjectures" in 1949. But the fact that he organized with Henri Cartan a group of mathematicians named *Nicolas Bourbaki* in 1935 in order to renew mathematics, and produced a series of new textbooks on the specialty named "analysis", shows better his critical attitude to the established.

To show his openness of mind to different worlds, I can cite the fact that he was one of the first Western mathematicians who discovered Japanese mathematical geniuses such as Kiyoshi Oka, Yutaka Takayama, Goro Shimura. Another fact that shows his extraordinary mentality is the application he made of group theory to a marriage system of an Australian indigenous ethnic group at the demand of his friend, Claude Lévi-Strauss. Obviously, he was discontent with modern Western civilization no less than his sister.

Simone and André were born to a non-religious Jewish family, which means they were quite distant from their ancestral tradition. In her last writing *L'Enracinement* (*The Needs for Roots*, 1943), Simone dealt with "rootlessness" (déracinement) as the most serious problem of modern civilization (Weil 3), but rootlessness just applied to her and her brother.

Now, rootlessness does not always work negatively. If one is aware of it, one may make use of it infinitely. In the case of Simone and André, it certainly isolated them from the rest of the world, but it allowed them to see the world from a universal point of view and discover a new horizon.

I said earlier that it was a shame that Weil did not know Teresa de Ávila because there is a spiritual kinship between them as Maurice Schumann, one of her friends, remarked (Henri Bergson et Simone Weil, 1993). Another important person she should have known better was Baruch Spinoza (1632-77), a Dutch philosopher of the 17th century. For if Teresa saw God "moving amid the pots and pans" (*Fundaciones* 5-8), Spinoza declared that everything in the universe is God (*Ethics*, 1677). They held a similar vision on the Divine Being. It is regrettable that Weil did not recognize her kinship in thought with the Jewish-non-Jewish philosopher.

According to Alain Goldschlager (*Simone Weil et Spinoza*, 1982), if Weil did not see the true nature of Spinozian philosophy, it is because it was introduced to her by Alain and Lagneau who saw nothing but rationalism in it. If she had known Spinoza better, she could have found sympathy with the philosopher who was expelled from Jewish community and condemned by the Church as "atheist".

Indeed, so far as the notion of divine creativity is concerned, Spinoza's thought was not far from hers although we should not overlook the fundamental difference between them. Spinoza's God was Nature herself that could be represented by "gravity" while Weil's God was something that went against "gravity". To her, the physical (=Nature) and the spiritual (=God) could not be together.

4

The reader of this article may still be wondering why Simone Weil was so hostile to algebra. Her insistence on poetry is not so difficult to understand, but her hatred of algebra may need more explanation.

As I said earlier, algebra emerged to humanity in Islamic civilization, the most advanced civilization in the Middle Age. Greek mathematics that had existed since antiquity was mainly geometric even if it developed number theories and analysis as well. Geometry means figures, perceptible reality, while algebra consists in abstract mathematical operations. It facilitates complicated calculation, by which one does not necessarily have to be engaged in it. It is convenient and efficient.

Algebra also has the special quality to unify different systems of mathematics by means of abstract symbols. It facilitates not only computation but especially generalization. Adopted by the European scientists of the 17th century, it surely gave a great leap to science, but of course, with the consequence that science itself became far beyond common sense because it left perceptible reality behind.

The question that emerges with this is if science can legitimately leave its perceptible basis or not? Most of scientists do not seem to care about it; on the contrary, they seem to be happy because algebra allows them to fly far away into an imaginary world freely. However, some philosophers are not satisfied with it, even horrified. Simone Weil was one of them. She regarded it as a big danger to human culture.

The first European who adopted mathematics in science is Galileo Galilei (1564-1642), the father of modern physics. But his mind was more geometric than algebraic. In an essay titled *Il Assigiatore* (*The Assayer*, 1623), he said:

> Philosophy is written in this grand book — I mean the Universe — which stands continually open to our gaze, but it cannot be understood unless one first learns to comprehend the language and interpret the characters in which it is written. It is written in the language of mathematics, and its characters are triangles, circles, and other geometrical figures. Without mathematics, it would be humanly impossible to understand a single word of it; without it, one would be wandering around in a dark labyrinth. (Galileo, 237-238)

As the quotation shows, geometry viewed by him was not a human invention but a property of Divine Nature. He saw mathematics in Nature.

Blaise Pascal (1623-62), a great mathematician and a religious thinker of the 17th century, thought of geometry as the center of mathematics. In his *Les pensées* (1670), he contrasted "*l'esprit de finesse*" (spirit of delicacy) and "*l'esprit de géométrie*" (spirit of geometry), from which we can deduce that algebra was not considered so much by him.

Things changed with René Descartes (1596-1650) who combined geometry and algebra to make algebraic geometry. With this, science, especially physics, made a great leap although Descartes himself was still attached to geometry. It is in the 18th and especially in the 19th century that algebraization penetrated deep in science. The degree of penetration was so high that physicists began to be unable to tell if they were seeking truth in Nature or mathematical coherence.

Just compare the following words of Steven Weinberg (1933-), a contemporary physicist, with those of Galileo quoted earlier:

> Science consists in seeking mathematically formulated and experimentally validated impersonal principles that explain a wide variety of phenomena. (Weinberg, xii).

It is obvious that Weinberg is thinking of explanatory mathematical formulae more than Nature herself. Moreover, he thinks that those formulae belong to scientists, not to Nature as Galileo thought.

The inversion of the position of mathematics from Nature to scientists happened in the 18th and the 19th century. In the time of Galileo and Newton, mathematics was believed to belong to Nature, and they revered Her as divine. Physicists posterior to them began to see mathematics as marvelous human invention that they could use to describe whatever they liked. What Weil found dangerous was that kind of science which had developed since the 18th century.

As everyone knows, algebra replaces the particular by the general. Its strength consists in generalization as I said earlier. Of course, generalization had already begun with arithmetic. For example, if we have two apples and then get three more, we finally have five, which case is to be expressed as 2+3=5. 2+3=5 is already abstract. But arithmetic is still connected to concrete cases and algebra is not. In algebra, a formula can be composed without any concrete number. For example, instead of 2+3=5, it may be formulated as "*a+b=c*" therefore "*c-b=a*". This tells nothing, no story, but it assures generality, even universality. You can put any number in the formula and it works.

Many scientists who use algebra must be happy with it because it allows them to go as far as to the imaginary end of the universe. However, there is a trap that they may not see or do not want to see. They may lose the sense of reality and become unable to see where they really are.

The next quotation is from a book by Masahito Takase, a Japanese historian of mathematics who points out the very problem of algebra.

Modern mathematics has something that the traditional Japanese mathematics called *wa-san* did not have: generalization of particular cases. *Wa-san* was a collection of particular cases, nothing more. (…)

Simultaneous equations is a good example of algebra. It is a system composed of numbers and signs that have no meaning. The theory to solve the question formulated in such equations is what is called algorithm that has no meaning or value. It is universally valid because it has no concrete meaning, because it is just abstract. It can apply to the traditional Japanese system and other systems equally. (…)

This abstract mathematics is easy to learn. To get to the solution, you do not have to have special genius, but just proceed from the basic principle as logic leads you. The way you walk on is the same way open to anyone. It is universal. (…)

Once you get used to it, you like its convenience and exactness. However, there is a problem, a serious one, there. It lacks in "joy of discovery". It lacks in catharsis. (…)

The abstract mathematics (=algebra) is like getting to the top of a mountain by bus that runs smoothly on a paved road. It is very convenient and fast but it is too abstract to feel you are getting to the mountain top. It is abstract because it is universal; in other words, anyone can do the same without much effort. You may even feel that it is not you who are going up to the top, but someone else. (Takase, 002-011)

As we see, Takase defines the universal and the abstract in algebra as "impersonal". It is this dehumanization effect that algebra brings about, and it is this that Simone Weil found dangerous. Just remember what she saw in factory workers; it was depersonalization.

Weil found algebra dangerous because it made science abstract, making distance between science and perception. As she thought that perception was the only source of our thinking activities, she found algebraic science capable of making us mindless and rootless.

Jean Piaget (1896-1980), a developmental psychologist, said that a prelingual child thinks by moving his or her body, using his or her senses. He called it "*l'intelligence psychomotirice*" (*La psychologie de l'intelligence*, 1967). He said in addition that this first stage of intelligence would be the basis of all human intelligence and it would last till the end of our life, but that with the acquisition of language, our thinking goes to the abstract, trying to combine perception with logico-mathematical intelligence. Let us imagine that our logico-mathematical intelligence goes alone without making efforts to combine it to perception. That is the case that Weil saw in modern science. To Weil, language and logico-mathematical intelligence should not leave perceptible reality behind.

This fear of hers has all the more value when we see that algorithm, the very product of algebra, is becoming almighty today with the development of Artificial Intelligence. This ultramodern device is an automatic thinking machine, which means it thinks instead of us. Does it really think? you may wonder. Some would say it does not because it is a mere machine. But it does think at least in algebraic sense. Weil insisted that such thinking was not real.

Now, some may think that A.I. helps us develop more creativity because it liberates us from tedious calculations. However, there remains danger in the use of such super-convenient devices. They are so powerful and so "intelligent" that we may deposit our capacity of thinking into it, which leads to the end of our creativity.

Returning to Weil, let us remember that her insistence on perceptible reality as the starting point of science came out of her ethical and religious vision of the world. We should not overlook the fact that she used the word "impious" to criticize modern science (Réflexions sur la théorie des quanta, 1941). She found it impious to think in logico-mathematical way alone, more impious to let algebra invade and dominate our mind.

As a philosopher, she did not take as much interest in modern philosophy as in science. Why so? It is because philosophy had become abstract, full of jargons that hardly anyone could understand. If Marx interested her, it may have been because the author of "*Poverty of Philosophy*" (1847) used a language that described reality in a perceptible way. She adored ancient Greek philosophy for the same reason.

Her attitude as to language in philosophy and science reminds us of Ludwig Wittgenstein (1889-1951). In his *Tractatus Logico-Philosophicus* (1921), we find a theory called "picture theory" intended to put limitation to the use of language. He insisted that we should not talk on things on which we cannot talk, and those untalkable things are notions beyond our perception such as God, good, evil, truth, beauty, etc. He warned us not to use such words because they described nothing. Weil did not seem to have known his philosophy although he was contemporary to her.

5

Let us have a closer look at Weil's writings on modern science. Among those, I will take only two: "Science et perception dans Descartes" (Science and perception in Descartes, 1930) and "Réflexion sur la théorie des quantas" (Reflection on Quantum theory, 1942). The two essays are longer than the others, the former being her first one on science while the latter the last one. Comparing the two, we can confirm that her point of view on science did not change much from the beginning till the end. She saw Descartes' introduction of algebra in science was the prelude to the catastrophe brought about by the emergence of quantum mechanics.

You may wonder if her understanding of modern science was correct or not. In my view, if her understanding was not always correct, her criticism possesses pertinence and value from today's point of view. The problems she found in modern science continue to be there.

The first essay "Science et perception dans Descartes" is composed of introduction, two main parts and conclusion. Let us examine them step by step.

The introduction begins with the comparison of Greek science and modern one. Weil appreciated Greek science based on geometry because of its direct connection to perception, remaining concrete and understandable to anyone. Among those Greek mathematicians, she chose Thales who gave birth to geometry. According to her, he brought about "democracy" to humanity.

> Thales discovered geometry, which was a revolution. This first one of all the revolutions was the only one that destructed the empire of priests. (…) He replaced it by the kingdom of true thinking. (…) His revolution also replaced inequality by equality. Thus, our duty became the one of obeying our own reason instead of the authority of scientists. (Weil 4, 3)

Her words "our duty became the one of obeying our own reason instead of the authority of scientists" sounds Cartesian. It is that attitude that she kept holding all through life. The fact she was not a professional scientist did not impede her from criticizing science because as a good disciple of Descartes, she believed she could judge it so long as she used reason.

On modern science, she said as follows:

> It is by modern science, by physics, that Thales' discovery was transported to the domain where perception was to be denied. (…) Thales would have been disappointed to see those geometric figures he had expected to find in the book of Nature became algebraic formulae. Science in the time of the Greek was the one of numbers, figures and machines, but now, it was merely the one of pure symbolic proportions. (ibid., 4)

She affirmed that there was no "figure" in modern science because it had cut geometry off, replacing it by algebra. According to her, algebraization means that science deals only with "proportions" that could be expressed in such a formula as $a : b = c : d$. She lamented that it did not deal with the concrete any longer.

The drastic change science underwent because of its algebraization means not only abandon of perception but also of "common sense", she added. Science could fly free to the "infinite" without caring about common sense, to which she manifested a total refusal. If physics became mathematics, how could it be physics? That was the question she posed.

To her, science was to discover truth, but that truth should be concrete and in concordance with common sense. This implied that it had to be useful to our life. Now, she saw many scientists contemporary to her having little interest in application of their studies. She found them irresponsible and unethical, and of course, she thought that it was due to the algebraization of science.

This criticism reminds us of Joseph Needham (1900-95), a great historian of Chinese science, who said:

> The sciences of China and of Islam never dreamed of divorcing science from ethics, but when at the Scientific Revolution, the final cause of Aristotle was done away with, and ethics chased out of science, things became very different, and more menacing. This was good in so far as it clarified and discriminated between the great forms of human experience, but very bad and dangerous because it opened the way for evil men to use the great discoveries of modern science and divert them to activities disastrous for humanity. Science needs to be lived alongside religion, philosophy, history and aesthetic experience; alone it can lead to great harm. (Needham, 7-8)

Weil attributed all those faults of modern science to Descartes who initiated the algebraization of science. At the end of the introduction of the essay, she said:

> With all this, I find it necessary to go back to the origin of modern science, to the double revolution by which physics became a sort of mathematics and geometry became algebra, in other words, to Descartes. (ibid. p.7)

6

The main part of the anti-Cartesian essay has two subdivisions. In the first one, the author enumerates Descartes' "errors", and in the second, analyzes the fundamental causes of the errors.

The first error she points out is the separation he made of the physical perceptible world from us by condemning perception as cause of errors. To her, without perception, we could not think of anything, nor could we make any science.

Descartes' emphasis upon reason was another error in her view, because it produced the illusion that we humans are independent from and superior to Nature. Arrogance and impiousness came out of it, she deplored.

And of course, his algebraization of science was the biggest error, she condemned. Because of this, the world became purely numeric, losing forms and colors. No one could breathe in such a desolate world.

There is a passage toward the end of the first subdivision in which Weil seems to have tried to rectify her position vis-à-vis the Father of French philosophy. There she confessed that Cartesian philosophy was not so simple as she had described, and that it had more nuances. Readers are embarrassed by the change of tone and cannot but wonder if she had some hesitation to carry on her criticism to the end.

Fortunately, at least to us, her rectification does not continue long. Soon she recovered her critical spirit to condemn Descartes as traitor to philosophy. For she said:

> How did he dare dedicate all his life to the studies of physics, he who adopted Socrates' motto "Know yourself"? (Weil 4, 31)

To end the first subdivision, she examined Descartes' famous "methodical doubt". She wondered why the doubt did not lead him to think that his existence was illusory. If he had doubted everything as he dared, he should have doubted his existence as well. Seeing that he did not do it, she concluded that his doubt was a "ruse" and that science based on such "ruse" could not be trustworthy.

Let us go to the second subdivision in which we find rare originality. Weil tried there to construct her vision of science to make clear the fundamental difference between her and Descartes. The originality comes from the spontaneity with which she developed her thought. She developed it as if she had been writing a confessional novel. It begins like this:

> We are living beings; our thought is accompanied with pleasure or

pain. I am in the world. I feel dependent on something exterior to me and at the same time, I feel that exterior thing is dependent on me. If I feel that the thing depends on me, I feel pleasure; if I feel dependent on it, I feel pain. All the things I perceive such as the sky, the sun, the clouds, the wind, the stones, are pleasure to me so long as they make me feel that I exist; they are pain to me so long as they make me feel that my existence is limited. Now, pleasure and pain are not totally separated from each other; they are mixed up just like in poetry. (ibid., 32)

The difference to Descartes is manifest there. She declared that she is "in the world" while he was not. This means that she would never lose perception nor feelings, which he was willing to do. She was convinced that she could not know anything without them, by which she condemned Cartesian worldview and science as false.

Now, what is interesting is that from this existentialistic declaration, she went directly to the question of mathematics. For she said:

Those things which are present to me are present only because I have the feeling that they are inseparable from my existence. (…) But I should not go so far as to conclude that I could not affirm anything beyond the feeling. It seems that abstract truths have nothing to do with the feeling; they have nothing to do with my concern about things. Arithmetic propositions are void of pleasure or pain; they are therefore easy to forget, but if I ever examine them, I find myself incapable of resisting their strict rules. (ibid., 34)

She asked herself if 2+2=4 is necessarily true or not and answered "no". This means that mathematics was accidental to her because it did not give any meaning to her existence.

We know that the basis of Cartesian philosophy and science is "*Je pense donc je suis*" (*I think therefore I am*). Weil challenged against this, saying the following:

> I never have consciousness of anything but appearances of the accidental. This thought is also accidental so long as I have consciousness of it. There is nothing more. (…) As for myself, I am anything so long as I have consciousness of myself. What my consciousness shows me is not me but the consciousness I have of myself. (…) I never know then what I have consciousness of. All I know is that I have consciousness. Yes, I know that I think. That is all I know. (ibid., 36)

She declared that her existence being accidental, no science could be of "necessity". There was nothing necessary anywhere, in her view.

This implies she accepted only the first half of the *cogito*, not the rest. She accepted that she "thinks", but she did not see the possibility to deduce her existence out of it as Descartes did because what her consciousness showed her was not she but the consciousness she had of herself. Only consciousness exists, there is no conscious being.

This position of hers reminds us of Buddhist theory of consciousness called "*Consciousness-only*" (*vijnapti-matrata*). Did his brother who knew Indian philosophy ever talk on it to her? We do not know.

Now, there is something strange in her thought. She started by affirming perception and feeling as real but affirmed now her feeling and thought illusory. Aware of the contradiction, she said that they were real only because she wanted them to be so. Yes, it is her belief that constructed the world. "I believe, therefore I am." That was her thesis.

Now, her focus moves from Cartesian *cogito* to geometry. Like today's cognitive scientists, she affirmed that geometry was born out of the illusion of our body action, and that it has been sustained by the common belief as being real. As for algebra, she affirmed that it is beyond "reality", impossible to "experience". She added to it that it could advance very fast because it did not regard us. Can such science propelled by algebra be "true"? That was the question she posed to herself. Needless to say, the answer was negative.

Then, what science was real to her? She insisted that the world was constructed by our body action, more precisely by our bodily work. The worker's vision proper to her is manifest there. Science should be a projection of worker's view upon the world, which reminds us of Marx's idea of production. In her view, it is by working that the world is made, so must be science.

There is no surprise then that she denied Cartesian notion of space named "*étendue*" that can be translated as "extension" or "area". If "space" is constructed out of a working body as she thought, the world will be full of meanings, but Cartesian "*étendue*" that totally neglects our working body cannot make any meaning to us.

We know Cartesian "*étendue*" has enabled science to be digital. The notion has allowed modern science to advance so fast and with incredible preciseness. Manifestly against this, Weil insisted on "*science du concret*" (science of the concrete) just as Claude Lévi-Strauss, her brother's friend, did (*La pensée sauvage*, 1962).

Against scientists who would say that they also use perception when they carry on observation and experiments, she argued that their perception was neither free nor natural because it was subordinate to the mechanism of observation tools. In addition, she asserted that they excluded any personal perception considering it as erroneous, which makes their science unreal.

Against scientists who believe that they can transform the world, she argued that they could not make any change so long as they depended on algebra that is incapable of giving any meaning to us. It is only by working with our body that we can change the world, she held.

Many of us may find her criticism on Descartes and modern science pertinent. However, surprisingly enough, we find a sudden change of direction toward the end of the whole essay. She began there to say that after all, science was necessary as a moral discipline. Without science, we might easily let our imagination and passion fly freely, which might lead us to disorder, she added. In short, she judged science useful for education although she found it unreal.

This sounds like a bad concession. We do not see why she needed to do it. What is worse is that she tried to attenuate her critical vision of Cartesian science saying that it was not so faulty as it appeared to be and that he tried to repair his errors by introducing God. This sudden mention of God is puzzling. We cannot but see there her oscillation between herself and France, her country where Descartes was considered as a Father-God. Can we conclude from this that she was after all a deracinated soul who desperately sought for a root in France?

7

Let us examine Weil's second essay "Reflections on Quantum Theory" (1942). It begins with the following words:

> Two notions brought about a deep gap between the science we have known since ancient Greece and what we call "science" today: relativity and quantum. The former made a sensation in the world while the latter is hardly known to us. Both were born at the beginning of the 20th century and remain subversive in the same manner by introducing an accepted and affirmed contradiction. (Weil 4, 130)

As we see, Weil saw "contradiction" in both relativity theory and quantum theory and she affirmed that the contradiction was "accepted and affirmed" by the scientists of her time. As contradiction is usually rejected by science, she found something extraordinary happening there.

As the title of the essay shows, she mainly focused on quantum theory, but before entering in its examination, she briefly explained what contradiction she found in Einstein's theory. According to her, the special relativity theory is based on the constancy of light velocity, which is incompatible with the principle of velocity measurement established in modern physics.

Not only she but many scientists of the time had difficulty in accepting the speed of light to be universally constant. But it was confirmed as true after many experiments and observations and Einstein's theory was put forward upon the confirmation. There was no contradiction in there.

Now, I personally find it regrettable that Weil did not take time to examine the theory of constancy in light speed. For "light" must have been of great importance to her. I also find it regrettable that she did not examine relativity theory more in detail, especially the general relativity theory, because the main theme of this theory is "gravity". As we see in her *Gravity and Grace*, the main subject of her theory on religion was also "gravity".

You may say that her "gravity" was not the same as the gravity physicists conceive. But why did she choose the term "*la pesanteur*" then? This French word is a term used in physics to mean a field that exerts attraction upon a body that has mass. Her intention was clear. She wanted to contrast physics and metaphysics by "gravity" and "grace".

Now, what problem did she find in quantum theory? First, she confessed that the notion of "discontinuity" it introduced to explain the basic structure of energy embarrassed her. It embarrassed her because she held that energy had to be "continuous" just in the same way as space or time. She saw there a rupture with common sense.

But couldn't we conceive a world of discontinuity as well as continuity? Couldn't we perceive the world in different ways at the same time? We do not need to choose one of them, eliminating the other. In physics, Niels Bohr (1885-1962) proposed to see the world in that manner by saying "*contraria sunt complementa*". In philosophy, Henri Bergson saw the continuous and the discontinuous as complementary aspects of one and the same reality (*Evolution créatrice*, 1905). Weil could have seen it likewise.

As a matter of fact, she saw it likewise. For in the same essay, we find the following words:

> What is more serious is that classical science dared to solve contradictions, or better to say, that correlations of contraries which make part of our existence and of which we are not allowed to get rid. Classical science dared to give solution to our fundamental condition by eliminating one of the two terms in opposition. (Weil 4, 141)

There she clearly manifested a view that contradiction was "our fundamental condition" and it consisted in "correlations of contraries" of which "we are not allowed to get rid". She did not refer to any god there, but it is obvious that she thought of someone or something superior to us who would not allow us to get rid of "our fundamental condition". She not only accepted but also needed contradiction for ethical and religious reason.

Following this view, Weil could have welcomed quantum theory, for this new theory gave a good solution to the problem she found in "classical science" that tried to exclude contradiction. If she did not welcome the new theory, what did she find wrong with it?

What she found wrong in it was its way of abandoning "classical science". She reproached quantum theory because this one did not establish any coherent vision of the universe by destroying the old one. However faulty it might be, "classical science" presented a vision, which left room for philosophical investigation. She saw no room left for philosophy in the new one.

One may think that her mentality was too old to accept the new science, but that is not exactly the case. The problem she found in quantum physics was shared by many physicists of the time. She would have welcomed the new science if they had established a new vision of the universe.

To her, what is wrong with quantum theory was its lack of reflection on its position vis-à-vis "classical" science developed by Galileo and Newton. To have a clearer idea of it, she took the trouble to review the whole history of physics. As quantum theory is concerned with mechanics, especially with energy, she focused on the development of mechanical theories on energy from ancient Greece till her days.

Her viewpoint as a historian was the workers' one as we saw earlier. To her, bodily work had religious and ethical connotations, which we already saw. The notions used in mechanics such as force, mass, heat, energy, were in her view all associated to the human body work.

From this point of view, she attacked quantum theory and Max Planck (1858-1947), its founder. She accused him of the "lazy" way he took to get to the conclusion. For she said:

> Planck introduced discontinuity in energy for the convenience of calculation, nothing more. (Weil 4, 135)

The word "convenience of calculation" is of extreme importance here because science in her view had to be inquiry of truth that should not depend on any mathematical "convenience". She found lack of ethic in Planck's physics.

As we saw in her criticism of Descartes, she was critical to scientific dependence on algebra. She found Planck's case worse. He was not only dependent on algebra but was looking for algebraic "convenience' alone. That is why she judged him unethical.

You may wonder if her criticism against algebra is legitimate from scientific perspective. It may well be so, for Richard Feynman (1918-88), one of the most brilliant physicists of the 20th century, lamented to see his colleagues absorbed in calculation and mathematical formulation. To him, science should not leave the concrete and the particular (Feynman, 3651/5405).

Weil blamed scientists of her time to be irresponsible as well. Examining Planck's following words, she condemned him as irresponsible:

> The author of a hypothesis has virtually unlimited number of possibilities; he is not limited by his senses any more than the instruments he uses. One may even say that he creates a geometry as he likes. (…) The most general conclusions that he draws out of the most sophisticated measurements he realizes may have nothing to do with real measurements. That is why no measurement guarantees the veracity of any hypothesis. It may offer however some unneglectable conveniences. (Weil 4, 138)

We know many scientists continue working with the mentality that Planck expressed above. The question of "responsibility" did not seem to worry them. Murray Gell-Mann (1929-2019), one of the specialists of quantum mechanics of the 20th century, is heard to have said "Nobody understands quantum mechanics, but it works miraculously well." If she had heard him, she must have been scandalized.

Now, even if she did not associate the development of quantum theory with any particular country, some historians of science have remarked that the symptom was more visible in hastily modernized countries such as Germany or Japan (Sasaki, 14-17). It is indeed in those countries that micro-physics made big success within a short time. Without having a solid basis of classical physics or philosophy that accompanied it, they absorbed science as an efficient instrument for their nations to develop the economical and military power within short span. What Weil saw as a serious problem in science must have been more remarkable in Japan or Germany.

Now, I hardly believe that quantum theory is a pure nonsense or danger. To us who live the 21st century, to deny it means to deny our life. We know we depend so much on it. Besides, as Claude Lévi-Strauss (1907-2009) asserted, the so-called totemism was a quantified system that works in terms of discontinuity (Lévi-Strauss, 296-297), which implies that quantum theory is a way of thinking lying at the bottom of our mind. We may have been quantum physicists without knowing it for quite a long time.

Now, after having criticized Planck harshly, Weil began to condemn scientists of her time as ignorant "village" dwellers. "Village" dwellers because they were confined in small departments named "specialties" in which they only communicated among themselves without listening to people outside. She accused them of never taking interest in what was going on in the world, not even in what was going on in science in general. Raised as "gifted children", they only possessed abilities to become "specialists" without cultivating anything important to be genuine human beings, she bitterly said.

What is worse, she added, is that they have greed and jealousy like anyone else, so they work hard to be first class scientists without any ethical scruple. As for society and the government that have no scientific knowledge, they just take new theories one after another for granted and choose some of them with the only criterium of "convenience" or "efficiency". Out of this is formed what is called "public opinion" that is almost always in favor of those ambitious specialists. Thus, unethical industry develops and spreads over to destroy the world, encouraging the public cult for science and technology.

Weil did not forget to point out their expression "Science says..." instead of "This is our opinion". She condemned it as evidence of scientists' lack in ethical scruple. She saw them shirking their responsibilities vis-à-vis society and humanity, on one hand, and imposing their theories as absolute truths, on the other. Seeing today's world, we notice that those expressions have not disappeared; they are present in internet, television and radio.

Indeed, the "irresponsible" system in scientific world she described is not gone. Let us have a look at the following words pronounced in 2015 by Sergei Nikolaevich Arteha, a Russian physicist who is examining the problems contained in quantum mechanics as well as relativity theory:

> When I was a student, I had a simple and romantic dream about the world and science. I often said to myself that the process of discovering truth was an extremely attractive one with such a variety of approaches. I thought of scientists as conscientious people ready to help each other to find out the best answer for us. I dreamed of "scientific progress" that sounded so beautiful as the solution for us humans to get finally in harmony with Nature. However, once I became a "scientist", I gradually realized that what interested most of the scientists were not the inquiry of truth but how to accede to funds or influential mass media, how to influence people, how to beat academic adversaries, etc. I also discovered that the only rule in the academic world was to "use any means to reach the goal". Since Perestroika, many scientists who became salaried workers have been thinking of how to sell themselves as attractive experts to clients, how to sell their labor to get as much money as possible, how to find a research project that may bring them a lot of money. (Arteha, 4)

What Weil feared in 1940's still continues.

As I said above, she saw the end of science in quantum theory, finding there no more inquiry of truth but only utility. She attributed this to the installation of "probability" which made science accidental, not necessary (Weil 4, 142). Probability makes "statistics" that can be justified only by "practical utilities", she said.

No doubt such science is ready to be used by political authorities or big capitalists eager to have money and power as she feared. However, we should not overlook the philosophical meaning contained in the notion of "probability" or "statistics" the value of which she did not see any more than Einstein.

As for technology that would develop with the new science, she had "no hope". She said:

> We have no hope as to the development of technology so long as we do not know how to impede men from using it to dominate others. As for our knowledge, we have no hope either about what is happening to science or technology because we are not "specialists". Even the so-called specialists hardly know about what is going on in other fields than their specialties. What they need is to stop and review what has been going on since the time of Archimedes till today. (ibid., 144)

As she pointed out, scientifically advanced countries of the time were making tremendous efforts to gather the newest scientific knowledge to use it for the domination of other countries. Seeing this, we find it important that she asked scientists to stop for a moment to make reflection on what they are doing. For it is the only way for science to recover the philosophical basis lost.

She warned scientists not to rush into complying with the request of their governments. As a matter of fact, not only totalitarian governments but also "democratic" ones urged them to do investigations for the victory and the prestige of their country, which hardly any scientist refused. Seeing all this, we understand why we cannot consider her thought out of date. The problem she clarified is still there in front of us.

As she said, modern science lost its roots because of the introduction of algebra. Just in the same way, industrialization and mechanization of work made people rootless. She knew that their rootlessness led them to adore techno-science and totalitarian systems. She saw that people stopped thinking due to the same cause. Algebra was a synonym to halt of thinking.

Her criticism of modern science that we have been examining was published only in 1966, more than 20 years after her death and World War II. This fact is regrettable itself because her contemporary scientists could not have a chance to listen to her. However, we can read them and learn a lot from them. We can still take them for warning. So long as the above quoted words of Arteha are valid, her criticism is valid.

Works Cited

Alain : *Propos sur la religion*, Paris, Presse Universitaire de France, 1969

Arteha, Sergei Nikolaevich : *Osnovania Physiki, Kvantovaya Mehanika* (*Grounds of Physics, Quantum Mechanics*), Moscow, Lenand, 2015

Bergson, Henri : *L'évolution créatrice*, South Carolina, CreateSpace Independent Publishing Platform, 2014

Coles, Robert : *Simone Weil, a Modern Pilgrimage,* Nashville, Sky_Light Paths, 2001

Feynman, Richard : *Surely You're Joking, Mr Feynman !*, 1985, Kindle

Galilei, Galileo : *Discoveries and Opinions of Galileo,* edition Text Only, 1957

Goldschlager, Alain : *Simone Weil et Spinoza*, Sherbrooke, Naaman, 1982.

Lévi-Strauss, Claude : *La pensée sauvage*, Paris, Plon, 1962

Marx, Karl : *The Poverty of Philosophy*, New York, International Publishing Company, 1992

Murray, Hanna : "Poetics of Labor: Simone Weil, St. Teresa and Mysticism" in *Invocations*, Bloomington, Indiana University Bloomington, https://invocationsiu.wordpress.com/2016/05/01/poetics-of-labor-simone-weil-st-teresa-and-mysticism/

Needham, Joseph : Precursors of Modern Science in *The UNESCO Courrier*, October 1988, https://unesdoc.unesco.org/ark:/48223/pf0000081712

Pascal, Blaise : *Les pensées*, Paris, Gallimard, 2004

Piaget, Jean : *La psychologie de l'intelligence*, Paris, Armand Colin, 1967

Santa Teresa de Jesús : Fundaciones, http://www.santateresadejesus.com/wp-content/uploads/Las-Fundaciones.pdf

Sasaki, Chikara : *Kagaku-ron Nyu-mon (Essay on Science, an introduction)*, Tokyo, Iwanami, 2012

Schumann, Maurice : Henri Bergson et Simone Weil, in *Revue des Deux Mondes*, Novembre 1993, https://www.revuedesdeuxmondes.fr/article-revue/henri-bergson-et-simone-weil/

Spinoza, Benedict: *Ethics*, New York, Penguin Classics, 2005

Takase, Masahito : *Kindai Sugaku-shi no Seiritsu, (The Formation of Modern Mathematics)*, Tokyo, Tokyo-tosho, 2014

Weil, André : *Souvenirs d'apprentissage*, Basel, Birkhäuser, 1991

Weil, Simone 1 : *La condition ouvrière* (Paris, Gallimard, 1951), en version numérique, Chicoutimi, Université du Québec à Chicoutimi, 2005

Weil, Simone 2 : *La pensanteur et la grâce*, Paris, Plon, 1988

Weil, Simone 3 : *L'enracinement*, Paris, Flammarion, 2014

Weil, Simone 4 : *Sur la science* (Paris, Gallimard, 1966) en version numérique, Chicoutimi, Université du Québec à Chicoutimi, 2004

Weinberg, Steven : *To Explain the World, the Discovery of Modern Science*, New York, Penguin, 2016

Wittgenstein, Ludwig : *Tractatus Logico-Philosophicus*, London, Routledge, 2001

Chapter 2

Claude Lévi-Strauss, an Integral Scientist

This article is meant to show that Claude Lévi-Strauss (1908-2009) was an anthropologist who tried to put forward a new science that would integrate science, myths, poetry and art. In my view, the science he proposed is what we need today for a better living on earth.

1

Although he is known as one of the most important anthropologists that ever existed, Claude Lévi-Strauss has often been considered as a philosopher. This is understandable because his works surely contain philosophical questionings which not a few people find valuable even today.

You may ask what philosophical questionings he made? what was his philosophical position? A good answer was provided by Paul Ricoeur (1913-2005), a French philosopher contemporary to him. After having read *La pensée sauvage* (1962), this one defined its author Lévi-Strauss as "Kantist without transcendental subject" (Ricoeur, 55).

By "Kantist without transcendental subject", Ricoeur meant a philosophical position that admits rational knowledge prior to experience as Kant did, but that differently from this one, does not recognize the existence of the conscious individual subject.

Kantian philosophy consists in seeing our knowledge as a synthesis of our innate cognitive system and our perceptual experiences. Kant asserted that we have an innate cognitive system thanks to which our mind can construct knowledge, classifying and associating perceptual data we receive from the world, and that our mind, the "subject", is independent from and transcendent to the world. As for Lévi-Strauss, he was certain that such cognitive system exists, but that it is not only structured by Nature but also by society, our mind remaining therefore within the world and dependent on it.

Indeed, Lévi-Strauss did not hold Kantian conception of human mind as a "subject" transcendent to the world. He rather succeeded the sociological view of his master Emile Durkheim (1858-1917), the founder of French sociology, who declared that "society is transcendent and immanent to an individual"(Durkheim, 74).

Holders of individualism would not agree to such view; they believe in the individual's absolute independence from society. To the sociologists such as Durkheim, that idea is nothing but a product of modern society. To them, humans become humans only by society. "*Nous sommes donc je pense*" (We exist therefore I think), that is their premise.

Let us remember the fact that our self-consciousness emerges with the word "I" which belongs to language that is a social product. And language is transcendent and immanent to us. Without society, without language, consciousness of our self would not have come into existence.

Now, even if the definition Ricoeur made of Lévi-Strauss' philosophical position was correct, he was wrong in taking the anthropologist for a philosopher. Being anthropologist means being a scientist of human societies and cultures who needs empirical evidence to confirm his or her view on them. Ricoeur did not see it.

Lévi-Strauss could have been a philosopher, but he chose science instead of philosophy. In other words, he needed material evidence to sustain his philosophical position. He preferred dealing with concrete data instead of abstract concepts.

Besides, what Ricoeur said about his philosophical position applies to many scientists. Scientists are more or less "Kantists without transcendental subject". They conceive Nature transcendent to us and their subjectivity totally obedient to Her laws. Look at Jean Piaget (1896-1980), the father of developmental psychology, Ilya Prigogine (1917-2003), the physicist that proposed "*la nouvelle alliance*" between natural sciences and others, Gerald Edelman (1929-2014), the neuroscientist who tried to open dialogue to philosophers. Their scientific spirit is exactly the same to our anthropologist's. All that Ricoeur said was nothing but to confirm that Lévi-Strauss was a scientist.

Lévi-Strauss is known for having made consistent structural analysis of human societies and their myths. His analysis is scientifically grounded, adopting methods used in linguistics, mathematics, physics, chemistry, even geology. It seems that Ricoeur did not see that aspect of his that made the core to his anthropology. *La pensée sauvage* is not a book of philosophy; it is a book of science.

Then why have many of us considered Lévi-Strauss as a philosopher? One of the reasons is our ignorance of science. Without a minimum of scientific knowledge, we could not appreciate his scientificity.

Another reason is that the very book of *La pensée sauvage* has a chapter in which the author defended his philosophical position attacking the philosophy of Jean-Paul Sartres (1905-1980), a philosopher contemporary to him. The chapter impacts us so much so that we have tendency to consider the anthropologist as a philosopher.

His criticism against Sartres may well be interpreted as a passionate

REFLECTIONS ON SCIENCE AND POETRY

defense of the so-called primitive mentality. In Sartres' *Critique de la raison dialectique* (1960), there is certainly an Eurocentrism that the anthropologist could not tolerate as wee see in the following quotation:

> One has to be very egocentric and naïve to believe that the whole humanity are confined in only one of the historical or geometrical model in which he or she finds himself or herself. Our truth resides in the fact that there are a variety of systems with differences as well as common properties. (Lévi-Strauss 4, 297)

However, we should not overlook the fact that Lévi-Strauss's assertion was propelled by a purely scientific spirit, not by a sentimental humanitarianism. For he insisted that history was not the only model to build up the science of humans; non-historical model was also necessary, and that Sartre's notion of history was lacking in relativity.

In *Tristes Tropiques* (1955) and other works of his, we find the same scientific spirit working. This does not exclude that he had poetical sensitivity, aesthetic eyes as well as deep philosophical mind, but the fact he was a scientist would not change.

2

No one would doubt that *Tristes Tropiques* is Lévi-Strauss' most literary work. Many would say that it is a beautiful autobiographical literature. "Autobiographical" is an adequate word, but I would rather say "confessional".

Although the book is full of ethnographies, we should say it is confessional because to the author, ethnography *was* confession. You may wonder how ethnography can be confession. We find the answer in his lecture on Rousseau given in Geneva in 1962 (Lévi-Strauss 2, 48).

Jean-Jacques Rousseau (1712-78) was the "philosophe" he adored above anyone else. His homage to the Swiss free thinker is found in the following passage of *Tristes Tropiques*:

> Rousseau, having the spirit of ethnology more than any "philosophe" of the time, had the most complete ethnographical documents one could have at the moment even if he never travelled far to the unknown lands. Different from Voltaire, he vitalized farmers' customs and people's thought with highly sympathetic curiosity. O Rousseau, my Master, O Rousseau, my Brother, I know we have been so ungrateful to you! I could dedicate each page of this book to you if my homage deserved your greatness. (*Tristes Tropiques*, Lévi-Strauss 3, 467)

It is rare to hear him speaking on someone so passionately.

Now, on the relation between ethnography and confession, Lévi-Strauss explained it in the abovementioned Geneva lecture by quoting Rousseau's following words: "I will do onto myself what a physicist does on the air to know its everyday condition" (Rousseau, 10). With this, he tried to show that Rousseau's confessional enterprise was a scientific research on himself.

The conception of confession Lévi-Strauss put forward is far from the one most of us have. We generally believe that confession consists in revealing one's hidden feelings or thoughts in which the confessors' self-identity is assured and that it contains much subjectivity. We do not see, consequently, any possibility for science to be born out of it. However, Rousseau's confession, at least after Lévi-Strauss' interpretation, was completely different, for the confessor's self-identity was objectivized and split into the confessing self and the confessed one.

You may wonder what all this has to do with ethnography. Lévi-Strauss affirmed that Rousseau who initiated the scientific confession was the most advanced ethnographer of the time and even the "founder of the sciences of mankind". In addition, he affirmed that what happened to Rousseau in making a self-portrait was quite similar to what happens to an anthropologist in making ethnography of a people he or she studies. Let us have a look at the following quotation:

> In each ethnographic experience, the observer finds himself (or herself) to be his (or her) instrument of observation (…), the ethnographer's self becomes thus different from the one who uses that instrument. (Lévi-Strauss 2, 48)

Let us imagine what an anthropologist has to do facing a social group he or she observes and describes. He or she is surely stranger to the group, but identification to the group even though imperfect is necessary because otherwise, the whole group would act unnaturally facing him or her. On the other hand, an anthropologist has to keep enough distance from the group to be able to describe them impartially. This is a hard task which may lead to the split of the anthropologist's self although it is the only way for ethnography to have scientificity. What he or she describes cannot but be confessional because he or she describes the part of his or her self which is identified with the object of description. In ethnography, science and confession become one.

In the same lecture on Rousseau, Lévi-Strauss did not forget to add that between Rousseau and him, there was Arthur Rimbaud (1854-91) who pronounced "*Je est un autre*" (*I is another one*). Without mentioning the poet's name, he quoted the poet's famous phrase to indicate that Rousseau's confessional science was an anticipation to Rimbaud's. The seed was sown by Rousseau, the plant grown up by Rimbaud and the fruit harvested by Lévi-Strauss.

As we saw, the ethnographer's split-self results from his or her efforts of identification to others that he or she has to observe and describe. Such efforts may be unnecessary in physical sciences in which objectivity and subjectivity are assured from the very beginning. However, if one wishes to enlarge the scope of science beyond the physical world, one will have to abandon that traditional set of subject and object. Lévi-Strauss who saw the limitation of the scheme naturally had a critical eye on modern science the very model of which is physics. In the same lecture on Rousseau, we find the following words:

> An ethnologist who aims at knowing humans needs to accept himself or herself within others first, but to realize it, he or she has to refuse his or her own self. This principle that is the only one any human science is based on, it is Rousseau who discovered it. If the discovery has remained inaccessible and been little understood for such a long time, it is because there has reigned a philosophy imprisoned in the erroneous conviction of the existence of "I" represented by Cartesian "*cogito*". The science that began with it focused on physics alone, abandoning sociology, even biology, aside. Descartes believed erroneously that he could pass from the inner world of self directly to the outer world of matter; he did not notice that between the two extremes, there were societies, civilizations, human worlds.
>
> (Lévi-Strauss 2, 48)

It is René Descartes (1596-1650) who was bitterly condemned there. The founder of modern philosophy was accused of having taken physics for the model of all sciences, abandoning other scientific possibilities such as sociology or biology. Modern science that has followed the path Descartes prepared was thus condemned.

Lévi-Strauss pointed out that Deacartes' fault came out of this one's "*Je pense donc je suis*" (*I think therefore I exist*). To the anthropologist, Cartesian *cogito* was egocentric and unethical. Science based on the *cogito* had therefore to be reviewed and revised. His anthropology was a trial of creation of another science, more complete and more ethical. I would call that new science "integral science".

3

I already said that Lévi-Strauss's criticism of Sartres was a criticism from a scientific viewpoint. Let us examine it more in detail to see what he really meant. The chapter in which he developed the criticism is titled "*histoire et dialectique*" (History and Dialectic). There, the author condemned Sartres' notion of "dialectical reason" as a symbol of the arrogance and egocentrism of Western intellectuality.

"Dialectical reason" was a common sense to many intellectuals of the West at that time, and it was based on historicism that viewed everything in linear historical perspective in which Western civilization was set as the top. Lévi-Strauss' criticism was focused on that historicism.

Karl Popper (1902-94) wrote "*Poverty of Historicism*" (1957) in which he attacked the same intellectual tendency, but he did it to defend liberalism and individualism from totalitarianism. As for our anthropologist, he condemned it as a symptom of unethical civilization. To him, history was a myth, the most powerful one, in modern Western societies (Lévi-Strauss 4, 303).

Most of the "civilized" people believed and still believe that history shows truth while myths tell lies. Historicism is certainly based on that belief. Lévi-Strauss criticized it to defend the "non-temporal", "non-historic" mind of the so-called primitives, but also to defend cultural relativism on which anthropology, his specialty, is based on.

According to him, anthropology allows us to see different cultures and societies that are "discontinuous" to one another. He condemned historicism because of its unilinear evolutionary perspective believed to be absolute truth.

This does not mean that he totally denied the value of historical studies; he recognized them as one of the necessary and efficient ways to understand humans. What he criticized in historicism is the groundless conviction that historical approach is the unique valid one. He proposed anthropology as another possibility.

He conceived history and anthropology complementary to each other. He defined the former as a study of humans in time and the latter as the one in space (Lévi-Strauss 4, 305). He knew very well that such juxtapositional view was no easy to be accepted in the Western world of his time.

He explained why it was difficult to accept it. He said:
> It is easy to explain their choice for history although difficult to justify it. The diversity of societies that ethnology captures in space present an appearance of discontinuity, so they imagine that history, thanks to its temporal dimension, can restore the continuity lost by ranging them as a passage from one society to another on the same line. And as we have tendency to believe that our personal change is continuous, we have preference for historical knowledge that offers us the sense of continuity. (Lévi-Strauss 4,305-306)

In history, he saw the illusion of "continuity" that he did not find in ethnology, and he knew very well that the illusion of continuity is far more powerful than the one of discontinuity because "we have tendency to believe that our personal change is continuous". The implication of this explanation is deep. He thought of the possibility for our personal change to be "discontinuous".

To him, "continuity" was just an aspect of our being; it can be "discontinuous" as well. Continuity and discontinuity were not incompatible but complimentary to each other. This view reminds us of the motto of Niels Bohr (1885-1962), one of the fathers of quantum physics: *contraria sunt complementa (opposites are complementary)*.

"Continuity and Discontinuity" was a question of viewpoint to our anthropologist. In *Le totémisme aujourd'hui* (*Totemism Today*, 1962), we find his deep sympathy with Henri Bergson's worldview. He defined Bergsonian worldview in the following manner:

> It seems that the proximity in worldview between Bergson and the Sioux comes from a same desire to capture two aspects of the real that the philosopher named "continuous" and "discontinuous", without choosing or excluding one of the two. (Lévi-Strauss 4, 145)

What is amazing in the quotation is that he found similarity between the worldview of Bergson and the one of the Sioux, a native American tribe. *Contraria sunt complementa* was an invisible tie that united him with Bergson and the Sioux.

4

I already said that *La pensée sauvage* is a book of science. All the chapters of the book show what science the author found in the myths and the magics of the so-called primitive peoples. The chapter that shows it best is doubtlessly the first one titled "*la science du concret*" (science of the concrete). Quoting a variety of ethnographies as evidence, he put forward a thesis that the so-called primitives are as scientific as modern scientists.

You may wonder if the myths and the magic of the "primitives" can really be scientific. For many of us have the impression that they are far from science. Lévi-Strauss opposed himself to such impression, insisting that they do have a science that has resulted from careful and patient studies of natural phenomena and that they have incessantly sought for laws and causalities behind them. Certainly, such a systematic and obstinate search of laws and causes deserve to be recognized as science.

Lévi-Strauss affirmed in addition that their studies are done out of purely intellectual interest, not of mere vital needs (Lévi-Strauss 4, 21). He insisted on it because he knew that there was a general tendency among the "civilized" to believe that only the "civilized" have purely intellectual interest in the world of phenomena. He wanted to overcome the widespread prejudice that the "primitives" do not make science because they are busy with their vital needs just like animals.

Now, if we admit the existence of science in the so-called primitive societies, we are not ready to accept that it can be as highly developed as modern science. Many of us have an evolutionary view that the so-called primitives' science, if ever it exists, is an unevolved or immature form of science. To this, Lévi-Strauss opposed himself proposing us to view that the science of the so-called primitives is another form of science that has as much validity as modern science, and that the two sciences have co-existed, collaborating with each other, even though it does not appear to be so.

To him, there were at least two kinds of science: science of the concrete developed among the "primitives" and modern abstract one developed in Western civilization. The former tries to find out an ordered system directly out of multiple perceptible data while the latter by way of mathematical abstraction. He found both sciences valid.

He knew very well that the "savage" science would never go beyond its mythical worldview, which he did not find faulty. For he said:

> According to Fletcher, an indigenous said "Each sacred thing has to be at its place" (Fletcher 2, p.34). This is a deep thought. And I could add to this that being at its place makes it sacred and that if ever one sacred thing were suppressed off the indigenous mind, their whole universe would collapse. (Lévi-Strauss 3, 22)

Obviously, our anthropologist defended the "savage" science that is profoundly related to the notion of the sacred, which we do not easily find in modern science.

Lévi-Strauss recognized science in the so-called primitive mind also because it constantly seeks causality behind the phenomena it observes. To this, he added that they try to apply causality to every phenomenon they perceive. As for modern science, he knew that it applies causality only to a limited area. We may conclude that the latter is more prudent and more efficient than the former, but he insisted that the "savage" science is science all the same because of its incessant quest of causality.

Lévi-Strauss' defense of the "savage" science with abundant evidence is eloquent and persuasive, but sometimes, we find it sophistic. For example, he said:

> Couldn't we go further to consider the rigor and the precision that we perceive in the magical thought and the ritual practices as unconscious apprehension of *truth of determinism* as mode of existence of scientific phenomena? Couldn't we think that determinism was *apprehended* and *practiced* before being *known* and *respected*? (Lévi-Strauss 3, 24)

This sounds sophistic because such extreme "determinism" that has no support of positive evidence is to be condemned as "superstition".

However, from his point of view, it should not be rejected as such. For there is a possibility for a "superstition" to be true when we find some evidence that proves it. Indeed, as Lévi-Strauss asserted, rejecting a "superstition" is anti-scientific; admitting the possibility of its scientificity is scientific.

Now, what is particularly interesting in the argument is his reference to a new tendency in modern science to "systematize all perceptible concrete data" just like the "savage" science does (Lévi-Strauss 4, 24). By the reference, he suggested the possibility for modern science to become "concrete" and nearer to the "savage" one. This is quite important for it corresponds to the very conclusion of the whole book of *La pensée sauvage* on which we will make reflection later.

I said earlier that Lévi-Strauss took continuity and discontinuity for two complementary ways of viewing the real. He did the same with the two sciences: the "savage" one and the modern one. In the chapter of "science du concret", we find his assertion that the "savage" science bloomed out in Neolithic Revolution the fruit of which we are still enjoying in form of agriculture, domestication of animals, weaving, pottery, etc. (Lévi-Strauss 4, 27). As for modern science, we know that it has been making enormous progress since the 17th century the fruit of which we are enjoying in many ways. The point is that he juxtaposed the two sciences in one and the same space instead of putting them in linear evolutionary order.

Indeed, juxtaposing two different things in one and the same space was quite proper to him. The origin of the juxtapositional view is found in the experience he had in his early days. The following passage of *Tristes Tropiques* reveals it:

> Among my dearest memories, I still keep the one of my pursuit of the contact line between two geological layers on the plateau in Languedoc. (…) All the scenery first showed itself as an enormous chaos that allowed me to choose the sense I would like to give to it. But beyond those agricultural speculations, geographical accidents, avatars of history and prehistory, there was certainly the august sense that preceded, commanded and explained other senses. That pale and obscure line, that difference of rocky debris hardly perceptible in form and consistence, witnessed two oceans that had existed one after another just at the arid land where I was standing then. (…) Indeed, sometimes miracle happens. On both sides of a hidden crevasse, we find two green plants of different species growing side by side, each one choosing the most appropriate soil for it. (Lévi-Strauss 3, 60-61)

The wonderful geological experience expressed here offered him the possibility to see the coexistence in one and the same space of two different species as well as "two oceans" that had existed in different periods of earth history. It taught him a marvelous notion of space-time which he learned not only by his intellect but also through his body.

5

It is an undeniable fact that Lévi-Strauss belonged to French sociological school founded by Emile Durkheim (1858-1917) and succeeded by Marcel Mauss (1872-1950). Our anthropologist published articles to show what he owed to each one of them. However, apart from Rousseau mentioned above, the one who influenced his intellectual formation most was Karl Marx (1818-83). From this one, he said he had learned that "social science is not constructed on historical facts any more than physics on sense data and that one has to construct a model and study its properties and behaviors in laboratory first, and then to apply his observations to interpret what is happening in reality" (Lévi-Strauss 3, 62). His structural anthropology came right from there. He studied human societies "scientifically" following Marx's method.

But do physicists really proceed as he described? Do they "construct a model and study its properties and behaviors in laboratories first, and then apply their observations to interpret what is happening in reality"? It seems to be so at least among the physicists of his generation. Abovementioned Niels Bohr for example said the following on quantum physics:

> There is no quantum world. This is only an abstract physical description. It is wrong to think that the task of physics is to find out how nature is. Physics concerns what we can say about nature".
> (McEvoy, 45)

Judging from this, physics is not objective positive science any longer; it has become something near to philosophy or literature even though it employs empirical methods that the latter does not.

To affirm the same, Richard Feynman (1918-88), another outstanding physicist of the 20th century, referred to "*atomic hypothesis*" in his *Lectures on Physics* (1963). He said:

> If, in some cataclysm, all of scientific knowledge were to be destroyed, and only one sentence passed on to the next generations of creatures, what statement would contain the most information in the fewest words? I believe it is the *atomic hypothesis* that *all things are made of atoms—little particles that move around in perpetual motion, attracting each other when they are a little distance apart, but repelling upon being squeezed into one another*. In that one sentence, you will see, there is an *enormous* amount of information about the world, if just a little imagination and thinking are applied. (Feynman, 9)

Hypothesis is used by physicists as an efficient model for a best interpretation of physical phenomena. They test it in order to make a law out of it. Feynman admitted that the existence of atoms is hypothetical as well as Bohr's quanta. Lévi-Strauss made science of humans in quite a similar way.

6

La pensée sauvage has attracted readers of different specialties because its explanations on the "savage" science cover different areas of our culture. In the chapter "*science du concret*", one of its most striking part is doubtlessly the one in which the author compared the so-called primitive mind to "bricolage". He said their myths are a sort of mental bricolage (Lévi-Strauss 4, 30). Readers are invited to stop there to think of the meaning and the value of bricolage that has normally been classified as a mere hobby.

The comparison becomes even more interesting when he contrasted "bricolage" to "engineering" and associated them to the "savage" concrete science and the modern abstract science respectively. Reading this part of the chapter, we can reach the essential of the "savage" science.

In Lévi-Straussian perspective, bricolage and engineering are two extremes: the former tries to make something out of the limited material at hand while the latter can, theoretically at least, make use of unlimited numbers and kinds of material judged necessary to carry out the initial plan. Obviously, bricoleurs' materials are "odds and ends" that used to be parts of something they had while engineers' materials are brand-new ones intentionally made for their purpose. Engineers can produce things they want or need as perfectly as possible; such enjoyment, bricoleurs do not have it because of their limited conditions.

Between the two ways of making things, most people today would choose engineering for efficiency and convenience, but Lévi-Strauss insisted that there is some advantage in bricolage that engineering does not have. It can offer human and personal taste because it depends on those "odds and ends" that used to be parts of something that remind the bricoleur of the past (Lévi-Strauss 4, 33). If the myths are product of the mental bricolage of the so-called primitives, the "savage" science deeply connected to them brings up a human taste that modern science cannot give.

Indeed, the "savage" science can give a meaning to our life because it connects everything to the world. To the so-called primitives, every single object is itself and the whole world at the same time, which makes their mind peaceful and stable. We cannot find such effect in modern science in which an object is an object, nothing more.

Lévi-Strauss tried to explain the difference between the "savage" science and the modern one in different ways. The comparison between bricolage and engineering was one of them. Another revealing way he adopted was semiotics. He explained the difference of the two sciences in terms of the different nature of signs that compose them.

According to him, the former, the "savage" one, is composed of signs each one of which corresponds to a constellation of concepts evoked by it just like in poetry. As for the latter, modern science, he defined it as a system of signs each one of which strictly corresponds to a concept (Lévi-Strauss 4, 32-36). The former is a polysemic system while the latter a monosemic one.

Lévi-Strauss adopted semiotics because he found it capable of explaining science, myths, art and poetry altogether. Thanks to this useful tool, he opened a way to "integral science" that I mentioned earlier.

Now, we know that semiotics is for the understanding of messages and that messages are the body of communication. If Lévi-Strauss viewed science and myth in terms of semiotics, it means that he viewed them as different ways of communication. This understanding helps us seize the meaning of the very last and the most important paragraph of *La pensée sauvage*:

> We have had to wait till the middle of the 20th century for ways of knowledge separated for a long time to meet: the way that accedes to the physical world by the detour of communication, and the way, recently discovered, that accedes to the world of communication by the detour of physics. The whole process of human knowledge becomes thus a closed system. (Lévi-Strauss 3, 321)

The conclusion of the whole book is right there in which Lévi-Strauss presented the very connecting point of the science that brought about Scientific Revolution in the 17th century and the science of the "*pensée sauvage*" that brought about Neolithic Revolution.

He defined the "savage" science as "the way that accedes to the physical world by the detour of communication", and information science as "the way, recently discovered, that accedes to the world of communication by the detour of physics". Their connecting point is "communication".

Let us notice that he did not have to deny modern science to defend the "savage" science. He was convinced that so long as we keep our mind authentically scientific, we shall surely reevaluate the way of thinking and knowing that once seemed to be "primitive". There again, appears the typical juxtaposition of his. He juxtaposed the "savage" science and the modern science on one and the same communicational basis.

7

We already saw that Lévi-Strauss set "bricolage" and "engineering" as two extremes, but we did not see that he put "art" in between. After having explained the difference between the two extremes, he started to develop his view on art, which allows his science to be even more "integral".

His view on art is quite original, for the main terms he used are "structure" and "event" that are not usually found in art criticism. He said for example:

> Art situates itself in the middle of scientific knowledge and the mythical thinking. Everyone knows that an artist is both scientist and bricoleur at the same time. A scientist differs from a bricoleur because the functions he assigns to "event" and "structure" are just opposite to those the latter assigns. The former creates "event" by means of "structure" while the latter creates "structure" by way of "event". (Lévi-Strauss 3, 37)

According to this, science creates "event" by means of "structure" while bricolage creates "structure" by way of "event", and as for art, he put it just in between.

But what does this really mean? We understand it better by replacing "event" by "discovery" or "invention", "structure" by "non-temporal universality". If art is between the two, it has to be inventive and particular on one hand, and non-temporal and universal, on the other. Art makes "event" like science, but it evokes aesthetic emotion thanks to being structural (Lévi-Strauss 4, 38).

Lévi-Strauss insisted that art gives aesthetic emotion by representing the structure of the universe in reduced dimension. Representing the structure in a small scale surely gives comfort and freedom of interpretation to a viewer as he asserted.

Now, if art is a pursuit of structural beauty of the universe, science also pursues the same. There is no surprise then that he finally asserted that aesthetic emotion is the common mother of science, art and poetry (Lévi-Strauss 4, 25-26).

Some may find his view on art too classical, too old-fashioned because it is based on the "structural beauty of the universe". But we should not forget that he was an anthropologist who saw the structural beauty of the universe as the source of aesthetic emotion commonly spread among many peoples existing on the planet today and yesterday. In my view, those who think he was old-fashioned should question if they are not imprisoned in modern museum-gallery art conception that tends to underestimate, for example, the aesthetic value of folkcraft.

8

Lévi-Strauss considered the "savage science" as incessant trials to "systematize all perceptible concrete data". That is why he defined it as "science du concret". I find it appropriate to compare the assertion of his to Gerald Edelman's neuroscientific theory. This one precisely insists that it is "science du concret" that the prelingual human brain tries to make.

Gerald Edelman (1929-2014), one of the representative brain scientists of our time, asserted that our brain thinks in metaphor before and after the acquisition of language. Here is a quotation of his words concerning the point:

> Being selective systems, brains operate prima facie not by logic but rather by pattern recognition. This process is *not* precise, as is logic and mathematics. Instead, it trades off specificity and precision, if necessary, to increase its range. It is likely, for example, that early human thought proceeded in metaphor, which even with the late acquisition of precise means such as logic and mathematical thought, continues to be a major source of imagination and creativity in adult life. The metaphorical capacity of linking disparate entities derives from the associative properties of a reentrant degenerative system. Metaphors have remarkably rich allusive power but, unlike certain other tropes such as simile, can neither be proved nor disproved. They are, nonetheless, a powerful starting point for thoughts that must be refined by other means such as logic. Their properties are certainly consistent with the operation of a pattern-selectional brain. (Edelman, 58-59)

What he meant is that because human brains are "pattern-selectional", they start to think in "metaphor" before the acquisition of language, but that the metaphorical thinking "continues to be a major source of imagination and creativity in adult life". There is no evidence that the neuroscientist read Lévi-Strauss. He referred to *Metaphors We Live By* (1980) of George Lakoff, a cognitive scientist, but this one does not seem to have read the anthropologist, either.

Now, what does "reentrant degenerative system" mean? For us to understand the term, Edelman offered quite a helpful metaphor:

> To help imagine how reentry works, consider a hypothetical string

quartet made up of willful musicians. Each plays his or her own tune with different rhythm. Now connect the bodies of all the players with very fine threads (many of them to all body parts). As each player moves, he or she will unconsciously send waves of movement to the others. In a short time, the rhythm and to some extent the melodies will become more coherent. The dynamics will continue, leading to new coherent output. Something like this also occurs in jazz improvisation, of course without the threads! (Edelman, 30)

This beautiful explanation leads us to see that our brain has a natural power to make its different parts with different functions concord and make up a unitary consciousness. It is those neuronal efforts to achieve concordance that Edelman called "reentry".

As for "degenerative", it comes from a biological term "degeneracy" which means "structurally dissimilar components performing similar functions". Each one of the brain parts that plays its own music has to renounce its original function to be in concordance with the others and that renouncement is called "degeneracy".

Now, Edelman's metaphor of "string quartet" or "jazz improvisation" leads us to think of the way people of different nature can get together to form society. Without pronouncing it, Edelman thought of the brain as a society, and that is exactly how our anthropologist saw the human brain. The following words cited from *Tristes Tropiques* show it:

I do exist, but not as an individual, of course. For what would I be if not an output of incessant fights between another society than ours composed of milliards of neurons sheltered under the skull and my body that works as its robot? (Lévi-Strauss 3, 479)

Although he did not see the body as another society, he saw at least the brain as a society.

A question remains. Is the brain a society similar to ours? For there is apparently hardly any such concordance or harmony in human societies. The so-called primitive societies may give a hint of the ideal social concordance, but our anthropologist stayed far from believing in such an ideal. The whole book of *Tristes Tropiques* witnesses a profound disappointment as to it.

9

Claude Lévi-Strauss was born in Brussels in 1908. His parents, Jews originally from Alsace, moved to Paris soon after the birth of their son. From childhood, Claude was a close friend to arts and crafts, not only of Europe of his time but also of ancient Far-East. His love of art and crafts was certainly fruit of the influence of his father who was a painter.

His premature appreciation of visual arts may explain how he got to conceive "structure", the core of his worldview and science. In everything, he found structure that evoked both scientific interest and aesthetic emotion. The following words of his in a TV interview with J-J. Marchand in 1972 show it:

> One day, lying on the grass, I was looking at a dandelion ball and thought of the organizing laws that necessarily presided on such a complex, harmonious and subtle arrangement. I said to myself it couldn't result from accumulation of accidents.

He referred there to the experience he had in 1940 on Maginot Line, the fortification built against Germany. He was sent there as a border guard, but obviously, his interest was not in the guard but in the structural beauty of Nature.

Let us remember that finding mathematical beauty in Nature and thinking of a law behind it is a Western scientific tradition. Galileo Galilei (1564-1642), one of the founders of modern science, said that Nature is a book written in mathematical language the meaning of which scientists have to decipher (Drake, 147). The marriage of aesthetic emotion and scientific interest is quite natural to scientists. Our anthropologist made no exception to this.

Now, when one speaks of structure, one cannot forget music, an extremely structural art. As is expected, Lévi-Strauss was a great music lover and confessed to having been a Wagnerian (Lévi-Strauss 3, 435). If he gave the titles "overture" and "finale" to the very first and the last chapter of his *Mythologiques* (1964-71) respectively, it is because he found profound affinity between myths and music.

As for poetry that is between science and art, we know that he carried out structural analysis on Baudelaire's *Les chats* with the help of Roman Jakobson (1896-1982), his friend who introduced him structural analysis of poetry. His aim was not to understand the poem better so much as to discover the position of poetry vis-à-vis myths. The conclusion he drew out of the analysis is the following:

> You may be surprised to see that an anthropological magazine publishes a study dedicated to a French poem of the 19th century. However, the explanation is simple: if a linguist and an ethnologist judged it good to unite their efforts to try to understand a Baudelaire's sonnet, it is because they found themselves, each one independently, in front of complimentary problems. Structures the linguist discovers in poetical works are amazingly similar to those of the myths the ethnologist discovers by analyzing them. (Jakobson, 5)

It may appear to be too audacious and hasty to draw such a general conclusion from the analysis of only one poem as they did. But we should not overlook the fact that Jakobson was expert in structural analysis of poetry and Lévi-Strauss of myths. Their conclusion that "they (myths and poetry) will substitute each other when their complementarity cannot work" (Jakobson, 5) should not therefore be judged as a simple "*coup d'intuition*".

Besides, Lévi-Strauss knew poetry quite well, at least French one. He loved Arthur Rimbaud, analyzed this one's sonnet "Voyelles" (Lévi-Strauss 5, 127-137), conversed with André Breton on beauty and originality (Lévi-Strauss 2, 22-23), associated *la pensée sauvage* of the so-called primitives with Alfred de Musset's song « Regrettez-vous le temps où le ciel sur la terre Marchait et respirait dans un peuple de dieux ? » (Do you regret those days when the sky was walking over the land and breathing in a people of gods? Lévi-Strauss 4, 318). If he did not allow himself to indulge in composing poetry, it is because he preferred being a scientist rather than a poet, which was also the case with Jakobson.

10

In the late 19th century, there emerged a group of intellectuals in France who started to take special interest in non-Western cultures and civilizations, among whom were Gaston Maspero (1846-1916) who became an eminent Egyptologist, Emile Durkheim (1858-1917), the father of modern sociology who extended his interest to the religion and the worldview of the so-called primitives, Lucien Lévy-Bruhl (1857-1939), the first philosopher who tried to understand the "primitive mentality" in philosophical terms, Sylvain Lévy (1863-1935) who became the leading specialist in Indian philosophy and Buddhism. Undeniably, many of them were Jews, on which we cannot but think that it was not a pure accident.

As there were certainly non-Jewish scholars of the same generation who took as much interest in "Oriental" civilizations or the so-called primitive societies, it would be imprudent to establish any theory on it, but it is quite probable that the intellectual Jews who were assimilated to Western society found themselves uneasy with the principles of their societies. It was natural then that they took interest in religion, philosophy or other cultural aspects in those societies beyond the West.

Among those Jewish intellectuals, Lévy-Bruhl and Durkheim had direct impact upon our anthropologist. Both had deep interest in the so-called primitive mentality. However, the first one's impact was received negatively, only the second one's positively.

La pensée sauvage clearly reflects the negative reception of Lévy-Bruhl upon Lévi-Strauss'part. The whole book, we may say, is a refutation of the theory developed by the former on "the primitive mentality". As for Durkheimain influence, Lévi-Strauss confessed that he owed a lot to this one in the article titled "Ce que l'ethnologie doit à Durkheim" (What ethnology owes to Durkheim, 1960, Lévi-Strauss 2, 57-62).

What were the points of Lévy-Bruhl's theory that provoked such a negative attitude in our anthropologist? To find them, we had better have a look first at the thesis Lévy-Bruhl developed in *Les fonctions mentales dans les sociétés inférieures* (1910). Here are the main points:
1) the "primitives" do not lack in logic or reasoning as Frazer or Tylor asserted, but they think "differently" from the "civilized";
2) the difference does not come from individuals but from the society that forms them;
3) the "primitives" have no aptitude for abstraction or conceptualization;
4) each "primitive" society has its "collective representations" that impose themselves upon its members on perceptional and emotional level;
5) those collective representations are not concepts, but "mystical" symbols that penetrate into the perception of the individuals that constitute the society; consequently, the "primitives" perceive nature as something natural and supernatural at the same time;
6) the "primitives" can think logically, but they rather obey "pre-logic" that is beyond the law of noncontradiction;
7) their "pre-logic" works obeying the law of "participation" by which everything in the universe is an item and a representation of the supernatural at the same time;
8) they can conceive causality, but their notion of causality is not

rational but mystical;

9) the rational knowledge of the "civilized" makes them distant from the world whereas the "primitive" mentality makes the "primitives" intimately close to the world.

I could enumerate more, but for our purpose, the above would be enough.

Now, even if *La pensée sauvage* was a total denial of Lévy-Bruhl's theory as I said, there are at least two points they had in common:

1) they both held that the "primitive mind" is never inferior to the "civilized" one;

2) they both followed the sociological view proposed by Durkheim who insisted on the transcendence of society onto the individual.

Seeing these, we cannot but appreciate Lévy-Bruhl because he asserted the theory above as early as in the early 20th century in which hardly any philosopher took the "primitive mentality" seriously. Let us remember that Lévi-Strauss' *La pensée sauvage* was published more than 50 years later than Lévy-Bruhl's book on the "primitive mentality". Lévi-Strauss walked on the path that Lévy-Bruhl had opened.

Some may think of Lévy-Bruhl disdainful of the "primitives" because he used the term "inferior" in the title of his book: *Les fonctions mentales dans les sociétés inférieures*. However, there is no passage in the book where he mentioned any mental "inferiority" of the peoples he called "primitives". All he said was that they thought "differently" from the "civilized".

Besides, unexpectedly enough, he thought of the "primitive" mentality present in a "civilized" mind. The following words we find in the forward for a Japanese version of his book allow us to see that his view was not so distant from Lévi-Strauss':

It would be an error to assert that such pre-logic mentality is only found among the primitives. I have tried to avoid such misunderstanding. Pre-logical mentality and logical one are never totally separated from one another. They coexist within a society, forming a structure, and it often or always remains within one and the same mind. (Lévy-Bruhl 2, 7)

Now, if both of them saw the "primitive" mentality in a similar way, what were the points that Lévi-Strauss criticized in Lévy-Bruhl? First, the latter's assertion that the "primitives" have no aptitude for abstraction or conceptualization. Lévi-Strauss quoted ethnographical evidence to show the contrary in the very beginning of *La pensée sauvage* (Lévy-Strauss 4, 11). Second, the word "mystical" that Lévy-Bruhl employed to explain the "primitive" mentality. Lévi-Strauss found it misleading because it would necessarily lead to the notion of the irrational. To him, the "primitive" thinking was as rational as the "civilized" one.

You may wonder how *la pensée sauvage* that relies upon myths and magic can be rational. The answer is simple: "mythical" and "mystical" are not the same; the first is ordinary while the second extraordinary. Lévi-Strauss insisted that *la pensée sauvage* that is mythical is just an ordinary thinking based on reason even if we are not aware of it. As for the mystical thought, it is beyond our rational understanding.

The third critical point is the "law of participation" that Lévy-Bruhl introduced to assert that the "primitives" perceive objects, beings and phenomena as they are and as something superior to them at the same time. Lévi-Strauss argued against this harshly, insisting on the following:

Their logic has double aspect, affective and intellectual. (…) Although they distinguish everything from other things, their feeling of identification with the beings they find superior to them is stronger than their notion of difference. (…) Their knowledge is just disinterested, careful, affectionate and tender. It would be superfluous to evoke there the bizarre hypothesis inspired to certain philosophers by an excessively theoretical view on the development of human knowledge. There is no room for the intervention of the supposed "law of participation", even less for mysticism coated with metaphysics. (Lévy-Strauss 4, 52-53)

Our anthropologist asserted that there is nothing illogical with the "primitives" who regard their object of study scientifically and affectionately at the same time because scientists in the "civilized" world, especially ethologists, do the same (Lévy-Strauss 4, 53-54). To him, Lévy-Bruhl was a philosopher who projected "mysticism coated with metaphysics" onto the so-called primitives.

There is no wonder then that he could not accept Lévy-Bruhl's term "pre-logic". To our anthropologist, those "primitives" are not "pre-logic" but just "logic". But if so, what difference in mentality did Lévi-Strauss see between the so-called primitives and the so-called civilized? He dedicated one whole chapter to answer the question: Chapter Two titled *Logic of totemic classifications*" (*La logique des classifications totémiques*).

His answer was based on semiotics. He took a semiotic standpoint from which he regarded the conventional logic and the "primitive" one as two different systems of signs: one composed of conceptual signs and the other of half-conceptual half-metaphorical ones. Remaining loyal to his principle of juxtaposition, he put the two systems as coexisting and complementary to each other.

Now, curiously enough, even if all the refutations Lévi-Strauss made against Lévy-Bruhl are justified, even if he made enormous contribution to the development of social and human sciences, we cannot help having the impression that the latter's "law of participation" or "pre-logic" have gained more popularity among common people than the former's scientific understanding of the so-called primitive mentality. We know that there have been many artists, poets, philosophers, fascinated by the "mystical primitives" that Lévy-Bruhl presented, but not so much by Lévi-Strauss' *"savage science"*.

One of the reasons of Lévi-Strauss' unpopularity comes from our ignorance of science. We know little of natural science, less of semiotics or information science so that we cannot understand Lévi-Strauss' point easily. As for Lévy-Bruhl's explanations, they seem much easier because he did not use any scientific term there.

Another reason is more fundamental. We prefer having "the primitive" and "the mystical" somewhere in the world. Lévy-Bruhl's description of the "primitives" just fits our romantic taste. A third reason may be Lévi-Strauss' infinite distance from the world. He situated himself as if he had been a stranger to the whole world, which we do not perceive in Lévy-Bruhl in any way.

That Lévi-Strauss chose to be far from any human society, everyone who reads *Tristes Tropiques* feels it. That distance he took allowed him to see human societies and their cultures as different systems of signs among which there was no continuity, but of course, the view is difficult to share for anyone. As for Lévy-Bruhl, he was a university professor in France till the end of his life. He perfectly functioned as a member of an academic institution. He was in the world.

You may say that Lévi-Strauss became professor in Collège de France. Once recognized in his country, he did enjoy academic success. However, we should not forget that he left Europe young and knew other worlds before he came back to have glory in his homeland. Academics such as Lévy-Bruhl always stayed in Europe without having the real experience of the globe. The difference between them is huge.

11

It was Durkheim who initiated Lévi-Strauss to sociology, but the one who really taught him ethnology was Marcel Mauss (1872-1950), Durkheim's beloved nephew. Our anthropologist confessed to the enormous intellectual debt to this one in « Introduction » to this one's *Sociologie et Anthropologie* (1962).

However, surprisingly enough, there is hardly any mention of Mauss in *Tristes Tropiques* in which the author tells the story of how he became ethnologist (Lévy-Strauss 3, 281). He insisted on his loyalty to "Durkheimian tradition" in the same book, which means that he followed the course prepared by Durkheim and Mauss, but it was only to defend himself from the "ungrounded" criticism in France according to which he was too much "Anglo-Americanized" (ibid., 64). We may doubt if Lévi-Strauss really felt Mauss close to him.

The loyalty he insisted on vis-à-vis Durkheimian tradition was true and not difficult to prove. If we compare "*De quelques formes primitives de classification*" reported by Durkheim and Mauss in 1903 and *La pensée sauvage* published in 1962, we see the latter's thesis as continuation of the former's. For example, when we find in the latter an assertion such as the so-called primitives do science by classifying objects, beings and phenomena, to establish "order" in the universe (Lévy-Strauss 4, 21-22), it corresponds to the following words of the former:

> Primitive classifications do not show any singularity or exceptionality even if they are so different from the ones used among the "civilized". Without any doubt, they are to be defined as the first scientific classifications. (Durkheim/Mauss, 42)

However, even if their intellectual proximity is evident, we cannot but see a ditch that separated them in quite a drastic way. It is not that they had personal problems with each other, but Lévi-Strauss left Europe to spend years in the New World while both Durkheim and Mauss stayed in France, enjoying their academic life assured by French institution.

I would not say that Lévi-Strauss suffered from being away from his homeland. He chose it and then benefited from it enormously. There is no doubt that thanks to the travels and stays abroad he made, he could have a wider worldview and a deeper philosophical insight. Without all this, he could not have become the anthropologist we know.

It is true that his extraordinary experiences with the indigenous in Brazilian Amazons and other peoples he met in different places of the world opened his eyes to understand humans. However, more important would be the fact that he was cut off the cultural environment he was used to. Travelling all over the world, he made himself solitary enough to feel stranger anywhere in the world. Without seeing this fact of his career and this aspect of his life, we could never understand his science. His science, we may say, is a confession of absolute solitude.

The whole book of *Tristes Tropiques* is a series of confession of such solitude, one example of which we can find in the seventh chapter titled "*Le coucher du soleil*" (*Sunset*) (Lévy-Strauss 3, 68-75). There we find the whole copy of the note he wrote on board for the new world, observing the sunset into the sea, a reading of which moves us a lot because we perceive deep solitude in which scientific mind and aesthetic sensitivity melt together.

As to the ditch between Lévi-Strauss and Mauss, there is an interesting anecdote in a book written by Louis Dumont, a Mauss' disciple anthropologist. There, recollecting his master, Dumont says:

> Mauss always talked walking. He would speak as if peoples in distant places or archives of ancient times had revealed him their secrets through conversation. Seated in the armchair, he travelled all over the world, identifying himself with the peoples he found in books. When he said "I eat", "I swear", "I feel", he meant "Melanesian people eat", "a Maori chief swears", "Pueblo Indians feel". (Dumont, 265)

This could never have happened to Lévi-Strauss who knew that identification to others would cost loss of one's identity. Mauss could "identify" himself to those peoples without pain because he met them only through books or magazines. As for Lévi-Strauss, he met them in their fields, and felt that those he was observing were observing him in return. To him, science of mankind had to be born out of such complex intersubjective experiences that could endanger his identity. Such science had to be a meta-science that views intersubjectivity as an object. It might have been comparable to relativity theory in physics.

12

Among the philosophers of all time, it was Lucretius (99-55 BCE) and Gautama Buddha (563-483 BCE) whose thoughts seem to have won our anthropologist's sympathy most. The epigraph of *Tristes Tropiques*, dedicated to Laurent, the author's son, is a quotation from Lucretius' *De Rerum Natura* that reads "*Nec minus ergo ante hæc quant tu cecidere, cadentque*" (*De Rerum Natura* III, 969), an English translation of which may be "*No less than you, those generations are gone, and the coming generations will continue to disappear.*" This immediately reminds us of Buddhist idea of "impermanence" and explains why Lévi-Strauss did not hesitate to confess his sympathy with Buddhist thought toward the end of *Tristes Tropiques*. We find the following words there:

> In fact, all I have learned from the teachers I listened to, the philosophers I read, the societies I visited, the very science the West is so proud of, were no other things than remains of the lessons that may reconstitute the meditation of the Sage beneath the tree...
> (Lévy-Strauss 2, 475)

Obviously, "the Sage" he referred to is Gautama Buddha, for it is well known that this one meditated beneath the tree of *bodhi* to have enlightenment.

The question is what Lévi-Strauss appreciated in Buddha's thought? The answer is given just below:

> All effort to understand destructs the object we have been attached
> to so that we may abolish it and continue to do the same with other
> objects; thus, we shall finally get to the only constant presence in
> which there will be no distinction of sense and nonsense, from
> which we had started. (Lévy-Strauss 2, 475)

If science is to understand objects by destructing them as physics has
been doing, Buddhist thought that he understood was science, nothing
more or less. As no science so far has ever reached "the only constant
presence in which there will be no distinction of sense and nonsense",
Lévi-Strauss dared to affirm that all sciences are nothing but tiny pieces
of Buddha's teachings. To him, the teachings made the science of sciences
that ends by denying itself.

But if so, shouldn't we abandon our sciences? No, for each step to
enlightenment is valid according to Buddha. Associating it to Marx's
dialectic view, our anthropologist expressed the thought in the following
manner:

> If the last moment of dialectic that leads to enlightenment is
> legitimate, so are the other moments that precede it or resemble it.
> (Lévy-Strauss 2, 476)

Returning to the notion of impermanence, Lévi-Strauss did not forget to
associate it to the physical notion of "entropy" as the following quotation
shows:

> From the very moment they began to breath and nourish themselves
> till their invention of atomic and thermonuclear power, except for
> their procreation, humans did nothing but eagerly dissociate millions
> of structures so that these became impossible to be reintegrated (…).
> Of course, they built cities, cultivated lands, but after all, those are
> nothing more than machines destined to inertia (…). Even the
> creations of their spirit have meaning only to humans and will be
> fused in disorder as soon as they disappear. It is legitimate to say

therefore that civilization is to be described as a prodigiously complex mechanism that tempts us to dream of survival of our universe, but actually, its function is just to produce inertia that physicists call "entropy". (Lévy-Strauss 3, 478)

This may sound pessimistic, but to him, it was juts real.

13

There are some who call Lévi-Straussian anthropology "counter science" (Sacrini, 2012). When one uses the word "counter", it means "opposite" or "anti", but of course, "counter science" does not necessarily mean "anti-science". The user of the word must mean another possible science by it.

Lévi-Strauss never showed himself against science; on the contrary, he always tried to be as scientific as possible. However, he was not satisfied with what most of us conceive as science. That is why he proposed a new science in the name of *la pensée sauvage*. If someone calls it "counter science", there is nothing wrong with it.

However, I would rather call it "integral science" because the science Lévi-Strauss aimed at was the one that would integrate natural and social sciences, modern and the Neolithic ones. Such science enables us to study myths, art, poetry, just in the same way as Nature.

By using the word "counter science", we could not express the integrity that Lévi-Strauss intended because the word necessarily indicates opposition, implying even a fight between sciences. Such oppositional view was inexistent in the perspective of our anthropologist; he always tried to find coexistence of different thoughts and cultures in one and the same space as we saw more than once.

Yet there is a problem in his science. Himself admitted that the question of the quantifiable and the unquantifiable was not overcome. He confessed not to having been able to get rid of certain impressionism (Lévy-Strauss 4, 85). This problem corresponds to the ditch difficult to bridge between the "savage" science and the modern one. It is still far from being intercommunicated.

Nevertheless, the fact that he proposed a new science despite the imperfection allows us to have a hope that the problem will be solved in future when the qualifiable and the quantifiable have easier communication between them.

The last question: we sometimes have the impression that his use of scientific terms is rhetorical. For example, he used the physical term "entropy" to explain some social phenomena, which may lead the reader to think of it as a trope.

The impression is wrong, however, for he did not use such words as metaphor in the sense we understand. To him, metaphor did not belong to poetry alone but also to science as Edelman, the neuroscientist, pointed out. Metaphor stays deep in our mind generating scientific concepts as well as poetical signs.

Lévy-Strauss was convinced of the interchangeability between scientific language and poetical one just like between the scientific mind and the mythical one. Science could not exist without language and language is necessarily metaphorical. Therefore, any word of science is metaphor, so is a word of poetry. When we understand this ultimate truth, we shall understand the whole of his science much better.

Works Cited

Drake, Stillman : *Discoveries and Opinions of Galileo Galilei*, Anchor, 1957

Dumont, Louis : *Essai sur l'individualisme*, Seuil, 1993

Durkheim, Emile : *Sociologie et philosophie*, P.U.F., 1974

Durkheim, Emile/Mauss, Marcel : *De quelques formes primitives de classification*, P.U.F., 2017

Edelman, Gerald : *Second Nature, Brain Science and Human Knowledge*, Yale University Press, 2006

Feynman, Richard: *The Feynman Lectures on Physics*, Vol. 1,Addison Wesley, 1971

Jakobson, Roman/ Lévi-Strauss, Claude: "Les Chats" de Charles Baudelaire, in *L'Homme* tome 2, 1962

Lakoff, George/Johnson, Mark: *Metaphors We Live By*, The University of Chicago Press, 1980

Lévi-Strauss, Claude 1: *Les Structures élémentaires de la parenté* (1947), Mouton, 1967

Lévi-Strauss, Claude 2: *Anthropologie structurale* deux, Plon, 1973

Lévi-Strauss, Claude 3: *Tristes Tropiques*, Plon, 1955

Lévi-Strauss, Claude 4: *La pensée sauvage*, Plon, 1962

Lévi-Strauss, Claude 5: *Le totémisme aujourd'hui*, P.U.F., 1974

Lévi-Strauss, Claude 6: *Regarder écouter lire*, Plon, 1993

Lévy-Bruhl, Lucien 1: *Les fonctions mentales dans les sociétés inférieures*, Hachette Bnf, 2016 ;

Lévy-Bruhl, Lucien 2: *Mikai Shakai no Shi-i*, translated by Yoshihiko Yamada, Koyama-shoten, 1928

Mauss, Marcel : *Sociologie et Anthropologie*, P.U.F. 1968

McEvoy, Paul: *Niels Bohr: Reflections on Subject and Object, Theory of interacting systems*, MicroAnalytix; Revision ed. 2001

Prigogine, Ilya/Stangers, Isabelle: *La nouvelle alliance*, *Métamorphose de la science*, Gallimard, 1979

Ricoeur, Paul : *Structure et herméneutique , Le conflit des interprétations*, Le Seuil, 1969

Rousseau, Jean-Jacques : *Les rêveries du promeneur solitaire*, Independently published, 2021

Sacrini, Marcos : L'Anthropologie comme contre-science. Une approche merleau pontienne, in *Chiasmi International* 14, 2012

Chapter 3

Haikai Poetry and Physics in Torahiko Terada

The subject of this article is a heritage from Akira Komiya, a friend of mine who had studied it for almost 20 years. With his sudden death in 2015, I started to read the papers he left on the subject, took keen interest in it, and decided to study it myself. The article below is a fruit out of it.

1

Torahiko Terada (1878-1935) was one of the most important physicists in Japan of his time. Yet he is known in his country as a scientific essayist more than anything else. His essays on science have been quite popular, some of which are still recommended readings at school. Written in simple and clear Japanese, they allow the reader to see what scientific spirit is.

His essays were not intended to propagate scientific knowledge to the public, but rather to show how a scientist approaches Nature. He showed it especially through detailed analysis of various phenomena in our everyday life. By reading them, we learn how to make science of the phenomena that surround us.

Generally speaking, it is rare that scientific essays give us a new perspective on our everyday life. They usually present science as something special, inviting us to praise its glory, or as secret keys for us to discover the marvels of the universe. Sometimes, they show us the personal life of a scientific genius, which does nothing but increase the mythological power of science. As for Terada's essays, they allow us to see what scientific spirit is and how important it is to view the world scientifically.

What we especially learn from his essays is the conviction that science is born out of our everyday experience and that it could not be separated from it. His essay on his travel to a volcanic province, for example, shows us how to read a geological history of the region through the stones and the rocks surrounding the volcano. In the same way, his essay on sweet candies called *confeito* shows the process of his pursuit of the cause of the geometric form of the candies.

That science is born out of our everyday experience is not a conviction belonging only to Terada. This is something that great scientists have repeatedly insisted on. For example, Richard Feynman (1918-88), one of the best physicists of the 20th century, confessed that he was disappointed at seeing his students unable to associate their scientific knowledge with the phenomenon they were just seeing through the window of the classroom (*Surely You're Joking, Mr.Feynman*, 1985).

As I said earlier, Terada's essays were not intended to propagate scientific knowledge to the public. For science was not readymade to him. Actually, he tried to show that science was not telling truth on Nature but a way of understanding Her. The following quotation from one of his essays shows it:

> For the moment, we do not know when we will have a bridge between life and matter. Specialists in biology and genetics are running after life in tiny cells. They are even making efforts to find a chain between parents and children in a chromosome. As for physicists and chemists, they are rather seeking life in a system of electrons existing in an atom, the tiniest element of matter. Among them, there are some who even believe in 'personality' in a tiniest

component of an atom… It is true that many scientists are making incessant efforts to explain life in terms of physics and chemistry, but I know on the other hand that many of the non-scientists dislike such research. They are just ignorant but ready to curse the day when a convincing explanation of life in terms of matter comes out. As for myself, I believe that if the day comes, it will be the day we will begin to see the real marvel of life. I am convinced that a material explanation of life does not consist in killing life; on the contrary, it opens our eyes to the essence of life that is filling the world of matter. (Six Springtime Episodes, 1922) (Terada vol.2, 225)

Instead of offering us a scientific answer to the question of life, which the common reader might expect, he just proposed a scientific way of viewing life phenomena and juxtaposed it to our common sense. We can understand from this that to him, science was a method and a proposal, not an answer.

The quotation above also shows that a physicochemical explanation of life that biologists might provide would not destroy but rather recover the animistic vision of matter that we have lost because of the spread of modern science. He tried to tell us that science was not to be feared because it could perfectly coexist with our common sense, even with religious faith.

His expression "a bridge between life and matter" shows that he thought of life as immaterial, but at the same time, he admitted that it could be studied as a matter and that there could exist a bridge between the immaterial and the material. To him, the premodern culture based on the notion of soul and the modern culture based on matter could perfectly coexist. He even thought of the possibility for us to have a complete vision of the universe by coupling the two.

Such a view may not have been shared by most of the scientists of his time. Even today, it would not be easy to be shared. Whether they stand for the modern civilization or not, scientists in general seem to believe that the mechanistic vision brought about by modern science has eliminated the animistic vision of the world. Terada's view was just opposite. He believed that the most "primitive" form of human thought could be revitalized by the most advanced science.

Such a view, he held it many years before the publication of Erwin Schrödinger's *"What is Life?"* (1944) in which we find the following words:

> The obvious inability of present-day physics and chemistry to account for such events (=life) is no reason at all for doubting that they can be accounted for by those sciences" (Schrödinger, 2).

Claude Lévi-Strauss (1908-2009) put forward a similar view forty years later than Terada. In *La pensée sauvage* (1962), the French anthropologist asserted that the most advanced science was ready to "evaluate the principles of the savage mind and to restitute it in the right position" (Lévi-Strauss, 321). By "the most advanced science", he meant information science of which Terada had no idea. Science of information had not been born yet when he was alive.

The common idea between Lévi-Strauss and Terada consisted in the possibility of the complementary coexistence of the two ways of viewing the universe, one dating from the prehistoric times, the other proper to the modern times. Let me quote the passage concerning it from *La pensée sauvage* :

> It seems that we have had to wait till the mid 20th century for the ways separated from each other for such a long time to join together: the one that accesses the physical world by making a detour of communication and the one that accesses the world of communication by making a detour of physics. The whole process of human knowledge gains thus the character of a closed system. (Lévi-Strauss, 321)

2

As I said at the beginning, Terada is known in Japan as a writer of essays on science. His readers know through them that he was a scientist, but not necessarily what scientific achievements he made. As for his haikai poetry, hardly anyone knows anything about it.

There is a concrete reason for people's ignorance of it. It is because his poetry was expressed in *renku* of which hardly anyone knows today. If he had made *haiku* or modern poems free of rules, he might have been better known.

What is called *haiku* is a modernized form of *haikai* poetry; it is attracting people still today. As for *renku*, another form of *haikai*, it is almost forgotten. That is why Terada is unknown as a poet.

What is *haikai*? We can say it is an aesthetic attitude. *Haikai* aesthetics consists in taking distance from the canon of beauty and parodying it. To do this, one has to know the canon quite well, but at the same time, one has to be ironical toward it. I would call it "aesthetic cynicism".

Haikai was born in the late 16th century and spread over the literary and artistic world during the 17th and the 18th century. It was the symbol of the end of the aristocratic culture that had been dominant on Japanese life since antiquity. It marked a new epoch in which plebeian culture blossomed out.

Now, *renku* was the commonest poetical form of *haikai* literature. It was a collective game played by several poets each one having to create a verse after the precedent one. Obeying certain rules, they ended the game by making up a long poem. They enjoyed the process of the game much more than the result.

In contrast, *haiku* is a solitary game. It was originally what was called *hokku,* the very beginning verse of a *renku* game. As time passed by, it became independent from the game to have its own existence and began to be called *haiku.*

The reason why it is more popular than *renku* in the modern times is not difficult to see. *Haiku* is more appropriate to a modern society where communitarian mentality is not influential any longer. Following Western models, the modern Japanese began to lose interest in keeping community by way of poetry, believing that poetry has to be expression of the individual and the personal.

Now, if Terada kept his interest in *renku,* not in *haiku,* it was not out of nostalgia for the past culture. On the contrary, he found possibilities, even future, in it. As a physicist, he absorbed Western scientific culture that marveled him, but this did not lead him to discredit the tradition of his own. On the contrary, it allowed him to rediscover the value of *renku* and *haikai* spirit which he thought to be complementary to modern Western science.

Let me quote a passage from one of his essays on *haikai.* There, he explained the value of *haikai* in the following manner:

> The Japanese seem to view humans and Nature as one and the same organism instead of separating them to establish a material and scientific attitude toward Her as Westerners do. Westerners conceive Nature as object and try to make use of it while the Japanese conceive it as a dearest brother or a part of their body. In other words, Westerners try to conquer Nature while the Japanese, at least the traditional ones, try to assimilate themselves or adapt themselves to it. (…) This difference of attitude to Nature has given science to the Westerners and haikai poetry to the Japanese. It may sound strange that I compare haikai with science, but you shall see it isn't if you see the essential of haikai spirit. (On haikai spirit, 1935) (Terada, vol.12, 226)

As the quotation shows, Tereda found *haikai* poetry as the very expression of Japanese view on Nature and added that it was equivalent to Western science that he defined as a typical Western way of viewing Nature.

This does not mean of course that he did not see the fundamental difference between *haikai* poetry and science. He did see it, but he did not choose one of them; he just juxtaposed them one beside the other, appreciating both. To most of us, science and poetry could not easily be put on one and the same ground, but he did it and gave them equal values.

You may wonder how he could see the equivalence of the two. He did not give an explicit answer, but we can guess it by looking back at the history of their formations. As is known, modern science is a Western creation based on the ancient Greek view on Nature. As for *haikai* poetry, it was born out of criticism of the ancient poetry that remained loyal to the prehistoric view on Nature. Seeing the two different cultural traditions, the Japanese physicist concluded that both were views on Nature each one having a long history and its own conceptual developments.

You may wonder what kind of view on Nature the ancient Japanese held? The best answer is found in the ancient poetry that started with *Kokin Waka-shu*, the first anthology in Japan compiled in 905 A.D. I will quote the beginning of the prologue of the anthology to show their view on Nature. It reads:

> Japanese poetry is made of thousands of word leaves coming out of seeds named human heart. People in the world, having a lot to do, cannot help speaking out what they feel and think by way of things they see or hear. Hearing the voices of spring birds among blossoms, hearing the songs of frogs in waters, who among all living creatures would not make a poem? Indeed, poetry is the only thing capable of moving heaven and earth without using force, touching even the demons' heart, making peace between men and women, calming the bravest warrior's mind. (*Kokin Waka-shu*, 9)

Those ancient Japanese defined their poetry as verbal expressions of the feeling and the thought by way of perceptible things.

We know through the poems collected in the anthology that the perceptible things in question were flowers, leaves, animals, linked to one of the four seasons. They were products of codification of natural phenomena that constituted a system of emotions. *Haikai* poetry that succeeded to the code system although it took distance from it did not forget to inherit the ancient view on Nature.

You may have already noticed that the quotation above contains a pan-poetic view. It says "Hearing the voices of spring birds among blossoms, hearing the songs of frogs in waters, who among all living creatures would not make a poem?" This implies a view that poetry does not belong to humans alone but to all the living beings. With this, we understand better why Terada saw *haikai* poetry as a view on Nature.

3

We saw that Terada tried to assimilate Western scientific culture without losing the traditional culture of his country. Just in the same way that he tried to complete a worldview combining modern scientific view on life and the animistic one, he tried to combine Western physics and *haikai* poetry. This kind of eclecticism may be traditional in Japan as is shown in the institutionalized juxtaposition of religions: Buddhism and Shinto. But I would rather associate it to the view on modern Japan proposed by Yukichi Fukuzawa (1935-1901), the leader of modernization.

This one declared that the modern Japanese had to live "two lives at the same time having one and the same body" and that there was no way of survival except for making comparison of the two which would allow them to have an objective view on the world that even the Westerners could not have (*Bunmei-ron no Gairyaku, An Outline of a Theory of Civilization*, 1875). Consciously or not, Terada succeeded to this spirit. He was ready to embrace science and poetry, physics and *haikai renku*, which he realized without falling into contradiction.

Terada chose *renku* because it was a collective game. He was a scientist and science is never a solitary game. It produces itself by following the precedent studies. Tereda who was used to working in such a way must have found himself more at ease with *renku* than *haiku*. You may say that *haiku* lovers also gather and make *haikus* in a group. But they never consider their works as products of the group.

There is another factor in *renku* that may have attracted Terada: aleatory nature of development of its games; *renku*, a collective poetry game, develops aleatorily. If this was the right reason, it is more important than the first reason I put above because one of the fundamental differences between science and *renku* is right there. *Renku* develops aleatorily without logic while science is supposed to advance logically.

You may wonder what the aleatory means in the development of a *renku* game. As I said above, each *renku* game is to make up a long poem, but the poem is not supposed to be a coherent whole. Each of the players of the game has to respect the general atmosphere of the whole, but that he or she is supposed to do nothing but adding a verse that suits the precedent one. There is therefore no direction, no premeditated destination.

You may say that such a game could not make any artistic work because a work must be a coherent whole. I would say that such way of viewing art is one of the possible ways, nothing more; art can be otherwise. If *renku* is an art even if it has no logical development, it is because it can evoke aesthetic emotion to the game players and the readers of their works.

Imagine a ball game. It has rules, but its development is unpredictable even though each of the plays is a consequence of the precedent. No one can predict how the game will finish. *Renku* as a game has such characteristics.

Of course, it is different from a ball game. A *renku* game has neither winner nor loser. All the *renku* players just enjoy the process of unexpected development of their game as well as each of its sequences. There is fun like in a ball game, but the aim is not the same.

I said *renku* does not develop logically. For example, the second verse that follows the first one must suit it logically, but the third one that comes after the second is only obliged to suit the second one without having to regard the logical coherence with the first one. It is natural then that the whole poem made of such verses does not present any coherent whole.

All that matters to the players of *renku* game is the process of linking verses one after another. It has no necessity nor preconceived plan, which is quite similar to life itself. Jacques Monod (1910-76), the Nobel laureate biochemist, explained that life process has no planning, no determined direction (*Le hasard et la nécessité*, 1970). We may say that *renku* is a miniature of life conceived as a process.

There is an essay Terada wrote about *renku* the content of which corresponds to all I have been saying. Its title is *Renku Zasso* (*Miscellaneous Thoughts on Renku*, 1931). There, he interestingly made comparison of *renku* with Freudian narrative of dreams. Let us have a look at a passage from it:

> Like a variety of elements that appear in a dream, the contents of each verse in a renku game is related to the player's multiple experiences hidden in the unconscious. It is usually the next player who unconsciously catches the unconscious thought network of his precedent and adds a verse inspired by it. Thus, the game develops on two levels simultaneously, on the surface level and the unconscious one. If by chance, the unconscious thought of the

verses touches the unconscious thought network of the reader, the literary effect of the game becomes greater. Differences exist however between Freudian dream narrative and the one of renku. Although they both develop by free association, a dream thought belongs to an individual so it does not necessarily evoke aesthetic emotion to others while a renku that belongs to a group of players has to evoke aesthetic emotion to them, even to the reader who is not playing the game together. (Terada, vol.12, 162)

It seems that Terada saw *renku* as a sort of collective dream developed by and composed of "free associations".

Let us have a look now at his practice of *renku*. He used to play the game with his close friends, namely Toyotaka Komiya and To-yo-jo Matsune. I will quote only the beginning part of one of their games published in a *haikai* magazine *Shibugaki* (*Astringent Persimmons*, 1927):

Matsune: From tomorrow on, I'll be going far into the north, wet in the spring rain

Komiya: Yet there remains snow on the mountain in the west

Terada: In a small village, I already see winter daphnes frozen

Matsune: The conduits in the garden have no entrance as usual

Komiya: An owl on a tree is calling at the moon of dawn

Terada: Happy though with fermented soybeans on the porridge in this chilly morning. (Terada, vol. 12, 36)

The first player Matsune began with "From tomorrow on, I'll be going far into the north, wet in the spring rain". Thus, he set the place, the time, the season and the atmosphere of the poem to be continued. Komiya, the second player, added to it putting "Yet there remains snow on the mountain in the west", changing thus the direction of the regard up to the "mountain", and by introducing "the west" in contrast to "the north" of the precedent verse, and mentioning "snow", he introduced a new space-time. The third player Terada, following the precedent verse, put his verse by referring to "a village" where "daphne" blossoms were still "frozen". As he set the scenery in a "village" and fixed the gaze to small flowers, Matsune, the next one, narrowed the scenery by putting "the conduits in the garden have no entrance". As "the garden" had no "entrance", Komiya, the following one, changed the tone of the precedent verse by putting "An owl on a tree is calling at the moon of dawn". Thus, he changed the direction of the regard together with time and space. To this, Terada added "Happy though with fermented soybeans on the porridge" to make the cold and lonely atmosphere warmer and more consoling. By mentioning "the porridge", he suggested a breakfast in an early morning of half winter half spring time in a remote village.

From the quoted part of *renku* alone, we can perceive the process that each of the three players, on receiving the previous verse, made another one, succeeding and renewing time, space, scenery, perspective, always respecting the atmosphere and the rhythm of the development. It is like movie scenes that develop continuously in which each sequence is supposed to be connected to the precedent one as natural as possible, but without making any coherent story. The important there is not to make a logical development but to keep harmonious atmosphere. You may say from this that *renku* is something between a sport game and art. Anyway, it is worth playing.

4

Physics as science began in ancient Greece, but physics Terada assimilated was modern physics that began with Galileo, Kepler, Newton. As a physicist, he knew very well that physics consisted in observation of natural phenomena, collection of data obtained through observation, analysis of the data, making a hypothesis out of it, testing the hypothesis by experiments in order to establish a scientific law, and finally, translating it in mathematical formulae.

Now, as we saw, Terada knew that physics was based on a view on Nature completely different from the traditional Japanese one represented by *haikai* poetry. He knew very well that the former set scientists distant from Nature so that they could observe it as an object while the latter invited people to feel being part of it. One could wonder if he did not find himself split between the two different ways of viewing Nature, but apparently, he did not have any problem with it, for he believed in the coexistence of the two and thought that combining them would lead to a more complete view on Nature. The following passage that I already quoted at the beginning shows it:

> For the moment, we do not know when we will have a bridge between life and matter. Specialists in biology and genetics are running after life in tiny cells. They are even making efforts to find a chain between parents and children in a chromosome. As for physicists and chemists, they are rather seeking life in a system of electrons existing in an atom, the tiniest element of matter. Among them, there are some who even believe in 'personality' in a tiniest component of an atom... It is true many scientists are making incessant efforts to explain life in terms of physics and chemistry, but I know on the other hand that many of the non-scientists dislike such scientific research. They are just ignorant but ready to curse the day when a convincing explanation of life in terms of matter comes out. As for myself, I believe that day will be the day we will begin to see the real marvel of life. I am convinced a material explanation of life does not consist in killing life; on the contrary, it opens our eyes to the essence of life that is filling the world of matter.
>
> (Six Springtime Pieces, 1922) (Terada vol.2, 225)

Terada began to take interest in physics in his high school days. Almost at the same time, he opened his eyes to the world of *haikai* poetry. There, in Kumamoto High School, he met a teacher of physics named Takuro Tamaru who introduced him to the world of mathematics and sciences. As for *haikai*, it was Kin-no-suke Natsume, a teacher of English literature, who revealed it to him. This one became a well-known novelist later with the pseudonym of Soseki. All this tells us that from his youth, Terada was a man who practiced the "two cultures". Quite young, he was formed to be a scientist and a poet at the same time, a modern man without losing his tradition.

What is remarkable is that he did not try to make a hasty synthesis of the two. Instead, he compared them to find out their connecting point. What distinguished him from most of his Japanese colleagues was right there. While these were busy assimilating Western science and culture without having time or space to look back at their tradition, he advanced his science without cutting his cultural tradition off.

Terada chose for example "Acoustical Investigation of the Japanese Bamboo Pipe, *Shakuhati*" as the theme of his doctoral thesis (1908). There, he tried to formulate in mathematical language the apparently irregular sounds of the traditional Japanese musical instrument, knowing that its sounds did not correspond to the scale of Western music. The key notion there was "fluctuation" that would be very important in physics later. Being loyal to the tradition, he was paradoxically on the way for a new science.

I already said that Terada's science was intimately related to everyday life phenomena. Except during his stay in Germany from 1909 to 1911 and just after that period, he almost always studied everyday life phenomena such as earthquakes, weather changes, geometrical formation of candies, irregular flows of black ink in water, etc.

Now, everyday life phenomena are concrete and perceptible, but irregular and evanescent while science of the time aimed at the constant, the regular and the unchangeable. In this sense, Terada was anticipating a science to come. He tried to discover regularity in those phenomena that repeatedly appeared in everyday life such as tides, earthquakes, geometrical forms of the angles of sweet candies, etc., and to do it, he applied "statistical mechanics" that was just sprouting in the West. In this sense too, he was anticipating the science to come.

Why did he take so much interest in finding out the regularity in those phenomena? There were two reasons: practical and aesthetic. Earthquakes, tides, volcano eruptions, were studied by him for practical reasons. He wanted his science to be useful for his country that had constantly been suffering natural disasters. As for the aesthetic reason, it is typically found in the abovementioned study on geometry in sweet candies' formation. Lover of music and fine arts, he wanted to understand the beautiful in everyday phenomena by way of science.

His interest in statistical mechanics may have been inspired by Ludwig Boltzmann (1844-1906) whose theories were known to him through his teacher of physics in Tokyo Imperial University named Hantaro Nagaoka. This one was a beloved student of Boltzman. But what is more important is that his application of statistical mechanics to everyday life phenomena anticipated Ilya Prigogine's thermodynamics.

Prigogine, Nobel laureate in chemistry in 1977, found that most of the "organizations around us" are characterized by their "dissipative structures" and that out of the "non-equilibrium" comes up "order". He asserted that the conventional physics and chemistry were only applicable to the "mean field" that would break down near "instability", but it was this "instability" that could originate a new structure. He called such structures "dissipative", affirming that they are the majority in Nature including human life. (Nobel lecture, 1977).

This was really an opening to a new science, a science that can cope with "instability" and "chaos" present in the commonest phenomena in our everyday life. This view, Terada anticipated it half a century before. He would have been happy if he had seen Prigogine's glorious development of thermodynamics.

It would be erroneous to suppose that Terada did not have interest in theoretical studies. He wrote a number of theoretical essays some of which we will examine later. I have to add to this that even though he took more interest in explaining quotidian phenomena in scientific terms than the rest, this does not mean that he had a utilitarian view on science. His interest was purely scientific, even philosophical; he wanted to know the truth of the universe hidden behind the world of phenomena.

The fact that he had scientific interest in natural phenomena familiar to us is manifest for example in the following passage of the essay titled "Mt. Ko-Asama" (1935). The essay is on the excursion he made to Mt. Ko-Asama, an active volcano in the province of Gunma.

> Up on the mountain, I saw many different kinds of erupted material scattered here and there, among which there was a deeply fissured volcanic bomb formed like breadcrust, presenting a multi-edged black minute surface. I imagined how it was made. A red-hot stone thrown up with eruption fell down on earth and its surface cooled down fast leaving the interior still hot. While the interior was cooling down, the gas within the stone came out like bubbles owing to the decrease of pressure coming from the exterior, making the interior loose like sponge and dilatating it. I suppose that the fissure was made because of the dilatation of the relatively hot interior against the relatively cool solid surface. It is often said that such fissure is product of a stone's shrinking due to its sudden cooling down, but that is not enough as explanation. We have to explain it in terms of the interior structure of a highly heated stone. I know many volcanic bombs have such an interior structure as I saw on Mount Ko-Asama. (Terada, vol.10, 175)

The quotation shows how he observed Nature and how he drew conclusions from the observation. As many scientists would do, he tried a structural reading of a textbook called Nature.

5

In 1909, just after the submission of the doctoral thesis to Tokyo Imperial University, Terada went to Germany and stayed there for three years to catch up with the scientific current in Europe. His main mission being to seize the most recent development of meteorology, he attended the classes of meteorology, geophysics, oceanology, but also the classes of theoretical physics given by Max Planck (1858-1947), the discoverer of quantum.

Meteorology, geophysics and oceanology were domains that interested him a lot because they were useful for his studies of weather, earthquakes and tsunamis. Japan being a country where typhoons and earthquakes are constantly damaging people's life, his interest in meteorology, geophysics and oceanology was quite natural. As for Plank's classes, he said he was fond of listening to the theoretical physicist because of this one's amenity in speech (On Berlin University 1909-1910, 1935).

His interest in theoretical physics surely increased during his stay in Germany. For after coming back to Japan in 1912, he began to study x-ray diffraction that was attracting some of the Western scientists of the time. Stimulated by Max von Laue's discovery in 1912 of the diffraction of x-ray shed on metal crystal, Terada started to investigate the cause of the diffraction.

It did not take him long to find that the orderly arranged structure of atoms in the crystal was the cause. Once he established the theory, he tested it many times and finally sent a report on it to *Nature*, the most prestigious scientific magazine of the time. The editorial board accepted it and published it in 1913. It was his first success as a physicist on the international level.

However, he was not the only one who discovered it. The Braggs, British father and son, studied the same phenomenon to find out the cause of x-ray diffraction without knowing or communicating with the Japanese physicist. The Braggs' report was also published in *Nature* in the same year, a little later than Terada's.

The difference between the Japanese physicist and the British father and son is that the former focused on the geometry of the atomic structure of crystal and reported the results of his experiments in plain English while the latter expressed their conclusion in algebraic formula. As the latter's way was the most appreciated form according to the convention of the scientific community, the Braggs' report had naturally more success than Terada's. They won the Nobel prize in 1915 while the name of Terada was to remain unknown in the history of modern science.

Terada's interest in geometry of crystal structure shows his aesthetic tendency. To him, algebraic formulation of Nature was less attractive than the perceivable beauty of Nature itself. Here, I remember Simone Weil's harsh criticism on Planck's physics. The French philosopher contemporary to Terada criticized it not only for being so far from "perceptible" reality but also for giving more importance to mathematical convenience than truth itself. She even feared that such abstract and hollow science could easily be used by a totalitarian system (Réflexions à propos de la théorie des quanta, 1940).

After the achievement in the study of crystal structure, Terada's scientific investigation shifted back to quotidian phenomena with which he must have felt more comfortable. Did he see that he could not compete with Western scientists skillful in mathematic formulation? It might be so, but the more important is that it did not mean a defeat to him.

One of the subject matters that interested him a lot was forecast of earthquakes. Himself experienced the big earthquake that attacked Tokyo and its suburbs in 1923. The government asked him to find out the cause and the necessary means to avoid the damage. He tried hard to find them out, but in vain.

What he found is that it was impossible for one scientist to find out the appropriate solution. He found it necessary to form a group of scientists of different specialties to carry on interdisciplinary studies because there were many different factors to cause an earthquake (Reflection on earthquakes, 1923). He lamented that there was no such research system in his country. Japanese government had followed the German model to construct universities in which each discipline was separated from others.

Now, if seismologic studies were his duty, his favorite was everyday phenomena such as flow of black ink into water or geometric formation of sugar candy called *confeito* as I mentioned earlier. He studied them scientifically, in which we find preliminary form of studies of dissipative structure or fractal mathematics that would flourish 40 or 50 years later.

Himself was quite aware of its value. In an essay titled "On periodic patterns in Nature" (1934), he said:

> Those phenomena I would call "statically natural periodic patterns" are for the most part put aside to the hidden corners of a countryside far away from the central cities where most physicists dwell in, so that very few of them have paid attention to them. But this very fact indicates the possibility for the "periodic patterns" to become an important subject matter in the future. The reason why they have not been studied seriously enough is that the classical methods of physics are not suitable to solve the questions posed by them. If ever we discover a suitable method to cope with them, those "strange and archaic" phenomena will surely be one of the central topics in the academic world. (Terada, vol. 7, p.70)

He was right in saying that the "periodic patterns" he studied in those "strange and archaic" phenomena would be an important subject matter in physical science in the future as the history of science shows.

Now, Terada himself judged his science "Japanese". It is understandable because the quotidian phenomena he took special interest in were generally phenomena that one could observe in Japanese everyday life.

His disinterest in mathematization of natural phenomena may also be attributed to his attachment to his cultural tradition. He who was a *haikai* poet must have found mathematization of Nature too "Western". To one of his disciples, he once said: "You don't necessarily have to follow the Western way of science; there must be a physics appropriate to the Japanese" (Uda Michitaka: Terada Torahiko, Father of Oceanic Physics, 1936).

6

I said earlier that Terada wrote many essays on theoretical physics. He wrote them after coming home from Germany. Let us have a look at two of them, namely, "On contingencies" (Guzen, 1915) and "On scientific laws" (Ho-soku ni-tsuite, 1915).

The reflections on scientific theory came up to him especially thanks to his reading of Henri Poincaré (1854-1912). This French mathematician and scientist who wrote beautiful essays on science fascinated him. Terada especially adored this one's "*Science et Méthode*" (*Science and Method*, 1908). He read its German translation and tried to translate one of the chapters into Japanese.

It is quite possible that he loved Poincaré's style because of its beauty and elegance. He must have found geometrical poetry in there even if he did not read the original text. As good writers in France would do, Poincaré knew how to express complicated ideas with precision and conciseness. We know that precision and conciseness are important elements in *haikai* poetry.

The following sentences the French mathematician pronounced must have been totally convincing to the Japanese physicist:

> Scientists do not study nature because it is useful; they study it
> because it is pleasant. Scientific research is pleasant because nature
> is just beautiful. (Poincaré, 15).

There in the quotation, we see the union of art, poetry and science.

Now, the abovementioned Terada's essay "On contingency" was directly
related to Poincaré's essay "*Le hazard*" (Contingency). One could even
say that it was an abbreviated translation of the latter. The question is then
why he chose it to translate? It is because his special interest was in
finding out regularity and constancy in apparently "contingent"
phenomena that belonged to everyday life.

Reading the essay, we find Terada quite convinced of the distinction
Poincaré made between the phenomena out of which one could draw a
scientific law and the contingent ones out of which one could not do it in
the same way. Interested in the latter, he must have felt sympathy with the
French mathematician who referred to the necessary emergence of a new
science. Reading Poincaré must have encouraged him to plunge himself
into it.

The other essay he wrote in the same year titled "On scientific laws" was
an extension of his consideration on contingency inspired by Poincaré.
But this time, Terada advanced his own view audaciously. He dared to
assert that what is called "scientific law" was abstraction of our concrete
experiences and that it could not be anything more than mathematical
approximation of reality by way of averaging its changes full of
contingencies and irregularities. The following passage from the essay
shows this idea in a clear way:

> Even if we humans demand Nature to be simple, She does not care
> at all. We can establish a law when She presents events with minimal
> complexity and changes. When on the contrary, events with enough
> complexity emerge, we consider them as 'contingent', which

Poincaré already pointed out. In most of the cases, we just average Her complexity and changes to make an abstraction of what She is. (Terada, vol.1, 145)

By saying this, he manifested a view that scientific approach to Nature that consisted in mathematization of phenomena was not sufficient.

As for the averaging of natural phenomena he found as a fundamental character of science, his critical attitude toward it is manifest even in the posterior essays. For example, in "Six Springtime Pieces" written in 1922, we find the following passage:

There is no relation between 'spring' as a season and 'spring' as a series of meteorological phenomena. Those occupied with making a calendar do not care about the average temperature of March in Tokyo. Seasons are a relative notion; for example, spring in the north hemisphere is autumn in the south hemisphere. Besides, spring does not exist everywhere; it exists only in some restricted areas on the earth. Everyone knows it but does not necessarily realize it. What is called the weather in Tokyo is therefore a result of the averaging of meteorological changes.

Averaging is justified because there is a cycle in it. But of course, the cycle changes every year. That is why we have to average the changes. What is important is not to believe in the average as the most probable or the nearest to reality. I insist on this because many people wrongly believe in the average meteorological conditions as real. As a matter of fact, we have very few days with such conditions. (Terada, vol.2, 224)

Here, we hear him warning. He warned us not to take the "average" for "real", not to believe in science as indicator of the real.

7

I have already mentioned the name of Ilya Prigogine whose scientific view on Nature was anticipated by Terada. The regularity and the constancy of irregular and chaotic phenomena Terada was seeking for were just what interested the Russo-Belgian scientist who won the Nobel prize in 1977 for his theory on the self-organization of chaotic dissipative system. In *La nouvelle alliance* (*Order Out of Chaos, Man's New Dialogue with Nature*, 1984) that he wrote with Isabelle Stengers, we find echoes of Terada's ideal of the union of the "two cultures". We see there a powerful proposal to bridge science and humanities as well as the studies of the imperceptible and those of the perceptible. The book begins with the following paragraph:

> Our vision of nature is undergoing a radical change toward the multiple, the temporal, and the complex. For a long time, a mechanistic world view dominated Western science. In this view, the world appeared as a vast automaton. We understand now that we are living in a pluralistic world. It is true that there are phenomena that appear to us as deterministic and reversible such as the motion of a frictionless pendulum or the motion of the earth around the sun. Reversible processes do not know any privileged direction of time. But there are also irreversible processes that involve an arrow of time. If you bring together two liquids such as water and alcohol, they tend to mix in the forward direction of time as we experience it. We never observe the reverse process, the spontaneous separation of the mixture into pure water and pure alcohol. This is an irreversible process. All of chemistry involves such irreversible processes. Obviously, in addition to deterministic processes, there must be an element of probability involved in some basic processes, such as biological evolution or the evolution of human cultures. Even the scientist who is convinced of the validity of deterministic descriptions would probably hesitate to imply that at the very moment of the Big Bang, the moment of the creation of the universe as we know it, the date of the publication of this book was already inscribed in the laws

of nature. (Prigogine and Stangers, xxvii)

As we see, the authors of *La nouvelle alliance* announced the possibility of the reunion of scientific and humanistic cultures by introducing the notions of "irreversibility" and "probability". Declaring the end of the timeless mechanistic classical science, they proposed a new science capable of taking in account "the complex", "the multiple" and "the temporal" including "evolution". Thus, they opened the door to interdisciplinary sciences in which not only physics, chemistry and biology could meet, but also social ones and humanities.

Such a wide and innovating view may have been possible only to scientists like Prigogine who was an outstanding pianist as well as an archeologist. Let us remember that our physicist Tereda was also of such interdisciplinary spirit. Apart from *haikai* poetry, he was a great lover of music; he even learned to play the violin.

Several years earlier than the publication of the abovementioned book, Prigogine already exposed his view on science in his Nobel Lecture in 1977. It began with the following words:

The inclusion of thermodynamic elements leads to a reformulation of (classical or quantum) dynamics. This is a most surprising feature. Since the beginning of this century, we were prepared to find new theoretical structures in the microworld of elementary particles or in the macroworld of cosmological dimensions. We see now that even for phenomena on our own level, the incorporation of thermodynamic elements leads to new theoretical structures. This is the price we have to pay for a formulation of theoretical methods in which time appears with its full meaning associated with irreversibility, even with "history", and not merely as a geometrical parameter associated with motion. (Time, Structure and Fluctuations, Nobel Lecture, 8 December,1977)

"Even for phenomena on our own level, the incorporation of

thermodynamic elements leads to new theoretical structures," he said. This suggested the possibility for us to reunite our everyday life phenomena and the most sophisticated theoretical science. For the first time in history of science, natural science saw the possibility to unite the "two cultures" the separation of which C.P. Snow denounced in 1959 (*The Two Cultures and the Scientific Revolution*, 1959)

Now, the notion of "history" Prigogine tried to introduce in science is one of the points that Terada insisted on. This one thought that science could be more exact if it had taken "history" in account more seriously. As early as in 1915, he already asserted that it was absolutely necessary to include "the historical" for science to establish a solid law. In the abovementioned "On scientific laws" (1915), he said as follows:

> Let's take the case of measuring the weight of an object with a spiral spring scale. If the constantly changing universe did not concentrate its effect upon the scale, we could not even have the notion of weight. The notion of weight or mass would lose its meaning. Besides, we have to take in account the effect of history on it. Not all of our scientific knowledge depends on the historical, but some, yes, depends on it. In the case of the spiral spring scale, we could not help thinking of the effect of the historical. To measure the weight of something, we should suppose that the elasticity of the spring will not change according to the temperature, the humidity, the barometric pressure that surround us, (…) but the biggest difficulty is the effect of the historical. In other words, each time we measure the weight of the same object with the same environmental conditions, we could not have the same result due to the effect of the historical, the influence of the past on the present. (Terada, vol.1, 148)

His point is that one could not establish any scientific law without taking in account "the influence of the historical" upon experiments. Science that did not take it in account would not be able to present any exact image of reality, he insisted. This idea remained lost for a long time until Prigogine retrieved it.

Other notions that unite Terada and Prigogine are "the irreversible" and "fluctuation". Among modern Japanese scientists, Terada was one of the first who gave much consideration to the second law of thermodynamics according to which the total entropy of an isolated system can never decrease with the passage of time and keeps constant only when all processes are reversible. In an essay titled "Notion of time, entropy and probability" (1917), the Japanese physicist said:

> I mentioned the irreversibility of time, but I must add to it that time is not equally universal. For there are systems with irregularity and disorder on the level of elements. If all the systems were 'divine' like pendulums, time could be reversible, but our universe is rather irregular and disordered so that it could not be described in terms of limited definitions and mathematical formulae. Certain scientists seem to believe in the possibility of predicting the future following the 'unchangeable' model of the present, but in reality, it is impossible except for some cases that satisfy certain conditions. That is why we need to think of probability and irreversibility of time. I believe that our notion of the present and the past derives from the irreversibility. (Terada, vol.1, 199)

Thus, he suggested that physics would have to start from the notion of "entropy". This is exactly what Prigogine pronounced in his Nobel lecture. Terada's scientific dream came true with the Russo-Belgian musician-scientist's new science.

Now, did Terada's understanding of 'the irreversible" and "fluctuation" have something to do with his practice of *haikai* poetry? To the question, I would say the following: those familiar with the traditional Japanese poetry like Terada knew quite well that its central notion was the constantly changing Nature with the irreversible passage of time. Irreversibility of time and loss of energy within a system were theoretically not difficult for those familiar with traditional Japanese poetry to accept.

8

Some essays Terada wrote are not on science but on his travel experiences, cinema, music, literature, folklore, etc. Among those, I would like to focus on one in which we perceive his trials to connect Western culture with *haikai* poetry, namely, "On cinematic art" (1932). For there, he dared to say that *haikai* poetry was "modernist". Let us have a look at the following words quoted from the essay:

> If hokku (haiku) should be a completed work itself, each verse of renku should not be so. It can only make a mental image when it is linked to the following verse. Renku is a sort of chain of verses composed of symbolic images residing in our subconscious. We may say that it is a more elaborated form of French symbolism or Edgar Alan Poe's poetry. In a way, those images chained one after another resemble a dream developed in a surrealistic movie such as "*Un chien andalou*" (*An Andalousian Dog*, 1928). (Terada, vol.6, p. 161)

Now, this has much to do with his comparison we already saw of *renku* with Freudian theory of dreams he developed in Renku Zasso (Miscellaneous views on renku, 1931). I will quote his words on it:

> Each verse in renku has its explicit contents chosen up by its author's personal experiences, but behind the explicit contents, is hidden the author's unconscious thought linked to the net of the unconscious thought prepared by the author of the precedent verse. The verse that follows it is also supposed to be linked to the net of the unconscious thought. Thus, the net of the unconscious thought spreads like a dream with each addition of a verse. (…) This way of developing renku surely corresponds to Freudian narrative of dreams, at least in part. The fundamental difference between the two is that the dream Freud analyzes is a personal and non-universalized one while the dream that develops in renku is a collective one that needs universalization to certain extent. (Terada, vol.12, 125)

The resemblance he found between Freudian dream theory and *renku* might need more careful examination, but it is certain that a *renku* game could not work at all if there were no transference among the players just as psychoanalysis would not work without transference between the analysist and the analyzed. There is certainly a link between psychoanalysis and *haikai* poetry.

9

I said more than once that Terada wrote essays on science not to propagate scientific knowledge to the public. He just expressed what he thought of science in his own words. It seems that he needed to do it for himself more than for others.

His essays served him as a bridge between physics he was engaged in and *haikai* poetry he was fond of. He wrote those essays freely, without obeying any rule that determined *renku* games or scientific articles. He needed to write something between poetry and science.

Was there any model for his essays? Henri Poincaré might have been one, but here, I would rather refer to Lucretius (99-55 BCE). For Terada loved this Roman philosopher's *"De rerum natura" (On the nature of the things*, the first century BCE) so much so that he wrote quite a long essay on it with the title of "Lucretius and Science" (1929). If Lucretius was not his model for writing, he must have been the source of inspiration at least.

Terada's essay on Lucretius begins as follows:

> More than ten years ago, I happened to read a book of history of physics in which I found the name of Lucretius for the first time. I was amazed to read the quotation in which Lucretius developed an explanation on the dusts in sunlight dancing without order. He explained it in terms of random movements of atoms, the small

invisible particles he thought of as the basic components of matter. I said to myself "There is nothing really new in this world, all thoughts existed already in antiquity." (Terada, vol.5, 18)

Terada confessed that it took him almost ten years since the moment he found Lucretius to begin reading him, but that once he opened the book, he could not stop it because he found so many stimulating things in there. "If ever I understood the whole book thoroughly, I would certainly find things and thoughts that no specialist of Lucretius has found yet", he dared to say, and added to it "I find there a plenty of intuitive discoveries that no scientist has proved yet" (Terada, vol.5, 18).

No wonder then that he enthusiastically recommended Lucretius to the youth who wished to be scientists. But unfortunately, these did not react as he expected. The following quotation shows his disappointment:

In a meeting with some young scientists, I introduced Lucretius' book as a must. One of them asked me then if there was any real significance in reading such an ancient work. I said "Yes, there is", fearing that such doubt was common to many of the scientists in our days. (…) Indeed, Lucretius' book is full of insights so that it may cast a new light upon the point at which we find ourselves lost. (…) What is science after all? What is exact science? The question itself does not belong to science; it is beyond scientific knowledge. Myself would not be able to find a good answer, but the problem is that today's students of science have no interest in such fundamental questions. They are sick and tired of so many pieces of specialized knowledge that they cannot have the slightest idea of what science is. (Terada, vol.5, 69)

The quotation shows us not only his disappointment but also his isolation from the other scientists of his country. If *De rerum natura* remained to be the very best text of science to him, the majority of the future scientists in Japan regarded it as a mere "literature", not a book of "science". The split between science, philosophy and literature may have existed elsewhere as well, but it may have been bigger in a country rushing in modernization such as Japan. There was hardly any room left for a scientist like Terada who remained loyal to the traditional spirit of science.

However, he had at least the luck to have some good students such as Ukichiro Nakaya who could follow the path he prepared. Those students, although not numerous, succeeded in realizing the poetical science that their master initiated. Indeed, poetical science is the suitable word to define Terada's endeavors, and his legacy is still there even today.

Works Cited

Baatz, Ursula : "Ernst Mach - The Scientist as a Buddhist ?"in Boston Studies in *the Philosophy and History of Science,* Vol.143, Springer, 1992

Feynman, Richard : *Surely You're Joking, Mr.Feynman,* Clive, Turtleback; Reprint edition, 1997

Fukuzawa, Yukichi : *Bunmei-ron no Gairyaku* (An Outline of a Theory of Civilization), Tokyo, Iwanami, 1995

Lévi-Strauss, Claude : *La pensée sauvage*, Paris, Plon, 1962

Monod, Jacques : *Le hasard et la nécessité*, Paris, Seuil, 1973

Poincaré, Henri : *Science et Méthode*, Paris, Flammarion, 1920

Prigogine, Ilya : Nobel lecture 1977, in https://www.nobelprize.org/prizes/chemistry/1977/prigogine/lecture/

Prigogine/ Stengers : *Order out of Chaos*, New York, Bantam Books, 1984

Saeki, Umetomo : *Kokin Wakashu* (Ancient and Modern Songs of Japan), Tokyo, Iwanami, 1996

Schrödinger, Erwin : *What is Life?*, Cambridge, Cambridge University Press, 2012

Terada, Torahiko : *Zen-shu (Complete Works)*, Tokyo, Iwanami, 1960-62

Uda, Michitaka : Terada Torahiko, Father of Oceanic Physics in *Shiso*, Tokyo, Iwanami, 1936

Chapter 4

Mathematics and Poetry in Kiyoshi Oka

1

It is often said that mathematics and poetry are intimately related to each other. Sometimes, we even hear that they are one and the same. But such audacious affirmation would need a solid ground, theoretical and empirical. By tracing the long career of the mathematician Kiyoshi Oka (1901-78) who said that mathematics is an art in which we draw our emotions on the canvas of intellect (Takase, ii), by analyzing his interesting comments on emotion, ideal, poetry, nature and mathematics, I hope we can have a glimpse of the ground.

First, I would like to illustrate, even if roughly, his career as a mathematician, then to examine the notion of "emotion" he considered as the source of mathematics. What he called "mathematical nature" and "ideal" will also be examined. Thus, we may approach the connecting point between mathematics and poetry. Now, this search is not irrelevant to the question of East and West. For his mathematics was surely fruit of the encounter of the two civilizations of which he was quite conscious.

Oka's specialty was what is called "theory of function with several complex variables". Those who are unfamiliar with mathematics can hardly imagine what it is. "Function" in modern mathematics means a relation between two series of numbers in which each element of one series exactly corresponds to each one of the other. For example, if there are two series of numbers, one composed of all the positive integers such as 1, 2, 3, 4, 5.. and the other of all the negative ones such as -1, -2, -3, -4, -5.., mathematicians call the correspondence "function".

Now, Oka studied "functions with several variables". In mathematics, the term "variable" signifies a changing quantity in one series that makes changes to the other series. If the first series has one "variable" within, the function is called "function with one variable" because there is only one "variable" that causes changes to the other series.

Let us imagine a case of a worker who is paid in proportion with his or her working hours. The pay for an hour is fixed so it is not "variable", but the working hours vary so they are "variable". In function of this, the total pay will vary, too. In that case, as there is only one "variable" that causes a change in the other series, their relation is defined as "function with one variable". Let us imagine that the pay for an hour changes after 7 p.m. In that case, there are two variables so the relation between the working hours and the total pay becomes a function with two variables. What Oka studied was more complicated. He studied functions with "several variables".

Now, what he studied was functions with "complex" variables. This means that his study took in account not only real numbers but also imaginary ones. This may sound extraordinary, but it was quite normal because in modern mathematics, numbers are always conceived as a complex of real ones and imaginary ones: "a" (a real one) + "bi" (an imaginary one). According to this, a real number is a particular case of a complex number that has zero imaginary one.

You may still wonder exactly what an imaginary number means. If the square of a number becomes negative, the number is considered imaginary. For example, if x^2 makes a negative number such as -3 or -4, x

is an "imaginary" number because it cannot be real.

But how did mathematicians come to recognize such strange numbers? The notion of real numbers existed since antiquity, but imaginary ones did not exist before Renaissance. It was conceived when some Italian mathematicians found themselves incapable of solving certain equations and felt obliged to introduce "impossible" numbers to solve them. Since then, with other mathematicians' approvals, those new numbers gained their territory in mathematics and in the 18th century, most of the mathematicians accepted the notion of "complex" numbers as a set of real numbers and imaginary ones. When Oka started studying mathematics, the notion had already been a base of mathematics.

Returning to the theory of function, the notion has existed since antiquity; we find it in the ancient Egypt, Greece, India, China, also in the so-called "primitive" societies. According to Claude Lévi-Strauss (1908-2009), the father of structural anthropology, what is called "totemism" is not a "primitive" religion but a sophisticated functional view focused on the correspondence between a series of social groups and a series of animal symbols or other symbols of natural world (*Le totémisme aujourd'hui*, 1962). If so, we can affirm that the notion of mathematical function is innate to human mind; those called "primitives" live it by their mythological belief while those called "civilized" learn it at school in math classes.

Now, why do we view the world in function? Because it is our nature, the French anthropologist would say. In the case of the "primitives", the functional view assures them harmony and union with their natural environment.

Lévi-Strauss also said that the "totemic" peoples' mind is metaphorical. If a series is in function of another series, it is natural that the one is conceived as metaphor of the other. Function can then be considered as a system of metaphors. As poetry being an art of metaphors, we can conjecture that the mathematical notion of function has the same origin as poetry.

We understand now why Oka who was specializing in the study of function said the following words:

> Mathematics is an academic art in which we draw our emotions on the canvas of intellect adapting ourselves to the form of what Western peoples call "mathematics". (Takase, ii)

Oka did not use the word "poetry" there, but we may safely say that the word "art" he used can be replaced by "poetry" because poetry is also an art to express emotions.

2

Oka's encounter with mathematics took place in his junior high school days. During a summer vacation, he happened to read a book written by William Clifford (1845-79), translated in Japanese. Clifford was a British mathematician known as a founder of geometric algebra. As the original title of the book *The Common Sense of the Exact Sciences* (1885) indicates, it was a kind of introduction of science for common readers.

There was one thing in the book that impressed the young Oka deeply: Clifford's circle theorem. The theorem looked so wonderful that it became a symbol of mathematical mystery to him. Later, in an essay titled *Shun-sho Ju-wa* (*Ten Spring Evening Talks,* 1963), he said:

> The theorem evoked awe in me. I encountered many different theorems later, which I tried to demonstrate for myself, but I have never dared to demonstrate Clifford's because I did not want to lose that feeling of mystery. You may know that a theorem loses its mystic value when it is demonstrated. (Oka, 20)

But for him to make the decision to be a mathematician, the encounter with Clifford's theorem was not enough. He had to encounter the theorem of Niels Abel (1802-29) who demonstrated the impossibility of algebraic solution of any equation of degree greater than four. This gave a profound impression to Oka, a young high school student. He thought that mathematics was great because it not only can solve difficult questions but also prove the impossibility of solving certain questions.

1922 was the year when Albert Einstein visited Japan. Many of his classmates dreamed of becoming physicists because of the event, but Oka said to himself that mathematics was "nobler" than physics because it could even show the impossibility of solution (Oka, 24). He decided to specialize in mathematics.

There was another reason for his choice of mathematics: "joy of discovery". When he was still in high school, he experienced a keen joy solving a hard question during the term examination. He cried out "I made it!" in the examination room, which must have surprised the rest of the class, but he did not care. To him, it was a "discovery", the first one in his life.

One may say that other students may also have solved the same question. But to him, it was a discovery all the same because he found the solution for himself. He left the school without sitting for another exam, went for a walk, lay down on a bench in a park and stayed happy there till the evening. We do not know what question he solved or how he solved it. What is certain is that the profound joy he felt at that moment motivated him to be a mathematician.

You may say that such joy can be found in other sciences as well. He knew it for we find the following words in the essay mentioned above:

> It is Archimedes who expressed the joy of discovery in the most eloquent way. He jumped naked out of the bathtub crying "Eureka". It was not to verify if his discovery was a right one or not, but just to express the joy of discovery. (Oka, 34)

REFLECTIONS ON SCIENCE AND POETRY

Now, there is a passage in the same essay that attracts our attention:

> Henri Poincaré, a great mathematician in Modern Age, wrote about mathematical discoveries with many details, but never referred to "joy of discovery". It seems that the more modern and sophisticated we are, the less joy we feel. If he never felt any joy in reality, it must have been because the education he received in France was already artificial. (Oka, 34)

We see from this that his understanding of "joy of discovery" was intimately related to natural assimilation of mathematics. He feared Henri Poincaré (1854-1912) did not experience such joy because this one might have been contaminated by an "artificial" educational system. He stayed a couple of years in Paris; he may have found the educational system there "artificial".

Now, let us remember his words quoted earlier:

> Mathematics is an academic art by which we draw our emotion on the canvas of intellect adapting ourselves to the Western form of what is called "mathematics". (Takase, ii).

This implies that to do mathematics, he had to assimilate "Western" form of expressing his "emotion". To him, mathematics was Western and that he was willing to participate in it even though he recognized himself as a non-Western.

On mathematics, he also said:

> What is called mathematics is a silhouette of a private and subjective mathematics projected upon an objective wall. (Takase, iv)

There he used the word "silhouette" which sends us to the notion of drawing or mapping. To him, mathematics was a drawing or a mapping in both of which cases figures and images play the primary role.

As for the "objective wall", he meant the abovementioned Western form by it. Projecting his "subjective" mathematics on the Western screen, he thought it would make something "objective".

I have already said that Clifford and Abel were mathematicians who impacted Oka deeply. As for Poincaré, he highly appreciated this French mathematician as the following quotation shows:

> If you study mathematics, you have to know what kind of intelligence you need to do it. I recommend you to read Poincaré's *The Value of Science*. There he said that we need to look carefully at the moment of mathematic discovery and that the moment is short but so decisive that one has the sensation of having no doubt at all. Indeed, such is the intelligence we need for mathematics. (Oka, 141)

However, we still have the impression that he was not totally convinced by Poincaré's mathematics. It may be because this one's words "the sensation of having no doubt at all" sound too Cartesian, too rational, to be emotional. To Oka, there would not be any mathematics without emotion. Although he found Poincaré's mathematics impeccable, he may have felt uncomfortable with it.

Now, apart from abovementioned Clifford and Abel, Western mathematicians who impressed Oka deeply were Charles Hermite (1822-1901), Poincaré's mentor who talked on the most abstract ideas as if they had been "alive", and Felix Klein (1849-1925) who did not hesitate to publish what seemed to him "emotionally true" even if he had not found a positive demonstration of it yet. Oka confessed to having bought three volumes of Klein's complete works and read only the articles in which Klein's intuition was splendidly manifest. As for Hermite, he confessed to having kept to himself the portrait of this mathematician as a secret treasure. He must have found an ideal in Hermite who regarded mathematics as poetry.

The name of Bernhard Riemann (1826-66) also appears in Oka's essays. This German mathematician was illustrated by Poincaré as a great "geometer" as the following quotation shows:

> Among the German mathematicians of the 19th century, there are
> two who are especially remarkable: Weierstrass and Riemann. The
> two found the general theory of functions. Weierstrass reduces all to
> the consideration of series and their analytic formations, or better to
> say, he reduces Analysis to a kind of extended arithmetic. Throughout
> his works, we do not find a single geometric figure. As for Riemann,
> just on the contrary, he quite often resorts to figures so that each of
> his conceptions is an image no one could forget once its meaning is
> captured. (Poincaré, 12)

There, Poincaré did not show any preference between the two
mathematicians mentioned above, but it is certain that Oka took much
more interest in Riemann than Weierstrass. For he never mentioned the
latter anywhere in his essays whereas the former appears more than once
as a great master.

On Reimann, he said the following:

> Riemann knew the ideal he held and tried to show that it was not
> imaginary but real. If you study mathematics, you have to learn his
> idealistic spirit. If Galileo raised up Reason to knock down dogmatism,
> Reimann idealistically showed the way to contemplate the eternal.
> Such spirit, you could never have it without humbleness... (Oka,
> 41)

Indeed, it was Riemann, the "geometric" analyst, that remained in Oka as
an ideal.

It is often said that modern "analysis" developed out of the studies on
"limits". This means that it started with "calculus", namely, differentiation
and integration that Newton and Leibnitz created in the 17th century. In
this perspective, it is natural to suppose that "analysis" is a study on
calculus and that the ancient analysis attached to geometry was completely
over in the modern age. However, abovementioned Reimann gave a new

life to geometry by combining it with modern algebraic analysis. Poincaré succeeded to it and opened a new mathematics named "topology". Setting mathematical objects such as points, lines, polygons, etc. in an imaginary space, this new field of analysis recovered geometry lost. Let us remember the keen emotion Oka felt at Clifford's theorem. The theorem would not have been born without Riemann's contribution. To Oka's analytical mathematics, images and figures were essential.

3

In 1929, Oka went to France to advance his studies in mathematics. According to him, he went to France hoping to find the "lifework topics". Having graduated from Kyoto Imperial University, he got a scholarship to study abroad and did not hesitate to go to Paris because he wanted to see Gaston Julia (1893-1978), one of whose articles had fascinated him.

Julia's article was on "iteration of functions" which means repetitive application of the same function. If a simple function is formulated as $Y=f(x)$, its iteration will be the repetition of $Y= f(f(x))$... Julia discovered that such iteration necessarily leads to chaotic values. Fascinated by this, Oka decided to go to France against the Japanese government's plan to send him to Germany.

Once in Paris, he tried to write an article on a problem relevant to iteration under Julia's direction. However, he did not achieve it because Julia told him that his perspective was "too small and too narrow". "A young man like you must go further and discover something completely new!" That was the French mathematician's precious lesson which reminded Oka of his starting point: "joy of discovery" (Takase, 68).

Fortunately, Oka found his lifetime topic before leaving France: "function with several complex variables" the studies of which had just begun in

Europe. As soon as he got back to Japan in 1932, he started investigating it.

In 1934, he found a "magnificent" book on the topic written by Heinrich Behnke (1898-1979) and Peter Thullen (1907-96). The title of the book was *Theorie der Funktionen mehrerer komplexer Veränderlicher* (*Theory of function with several complex variables* 1934). The book stimulated him so much so that he worked hard to make something new in the field, and finally in 1936, he wrote the first article on the topic in French. Since then, he continued writing articles on it always in French, each time from a different angle. In 1961, he published a book that collected all the articles on the subject the title of which was *Sur les fonctions analytiques de plusieurs variables*.

He published his works in French because at that time, there were no Japanese who could follow him well while in France, there were mathematicians such as Henri Cartan (1904-2008) investigating the same topic. Besides, he felt more comfortable in writing French than other languages because he learned how to write an article in France.

In 1938, he sent copies of his third article to Behnke and Cartan. Both of these were much impressed by the article and sent him a postcard immediately after. However, Oka received it a year later because he had lost job in Hiroshima Imperial University to which they had sent it. Even so, our mathematician must have felt great joy to find the beautiful words in the card as follows:

> We read your article on Cousin's problems (the third article), which we found marvelous, but there remains a question. Should we pronounce your name Oka as a French would do? or Okay as an American would do? (Takase, 146)

In such humorous and affectionate words, we perceive a genuine academic friendship beyond nations. It would be useful to point it out that at that moment, Germany was to invade Poland and Japan was to militarize the whole nation making alliance with Fascist Germany and Italy.

After the war, in 1948, Oka sent his seventh article to Cartan, but by way of André Weil (1906-98) who was in the U.S. It was not easy to send a courier from Japan to Europe directly in that period of postwar. Weil, the elder brother of Simone Weil, was an eminent mathematician who created with Cartan a group of mathematicians named Nicolas Bourbaki. After having read and appreciated Oka's work, he sent it to his friend Cartan in Paris, and this one published it in *Le Bulletin de la Société Mathématique de France* in 1950.

Since then, Oka became a bit famous among Western mathematicians, some of whom even went to Japan to visit him. The first visitor was Jean-Pierre Serre, Cartan's disciple, the second one above-mentioned Weil. And the third, Carl Siegel (1896-1981), visited him three years later, feeling deep sympathy with the Japanese mathematician because of this one's following words in his 10th article:

> I would like to express my feeling about the tendency of our mathematics today. I allow myself to express it in terms of seasonal sense which derives from the ancient tradition of the Japanese. I find today's mathematics going abstract, too abstract. The theorems in our field have become too much general, some of them showing no relevance to the space of "complex variables". We are in winter, I would say. I have been waiting for spring to come for a long time, wishing to do some work that may give a sense of spring. The present work is the first fruit of my wish. (Takase, 202)

Siegel was happy to find such a view of the Japanese mathematician, for he found his contemporary mathematicians like "pigs intruding onto the beautiful garden carefully taken care of by Gauss, Lagrange, etc." (Takase, 201). When he saw Oka in person, he could not stop hugging him warmly.

Cartan who was the closest to Oka from mathematical point of view met the Japanese mathematician later. But before that, he had already shown deep respect to him saying the following in one of his articles:

> The Japanese mathematician named Oka investigated the same problems as myself, completely independently from me. His beautiful articles that preceded mine led me to study the question of "ideal" in analytic functions. Away from here in Europe, without being able to know what I was doing with the "ideal", he wrote an article on the same topic in 1948, which brought much more fruit than mine written in 1944. (Takase, 206-207)

The term "ideal" in the quotation has a specific meaning in mathematics; it means a subset of an algebraic structure.

It is known that Oka's investigation of functions with several variables owed a lot to Cartan's works. Exchanging their works to each other, they communicated and established a beautiful friendship. Oka used to say to his friends "Cartan is the one I miss".

Now, knowing all this, the following comment Oka made about Cartan's latest works is a bit surprising. Toward the end of his life, he said as follows:

> I read Cartan's recent works and found his mathematics impoverished. It seems all that matters to him is to draw out a new result. (…) There I saw the difference between those who hold an eternal ideal and those who do not. (Takase, 188)

In Cartan, he found the lack of ideal that he found for example in Riemann. To him, mathematicians should always be in pursuit of ideal. Needless to say, this ideal is not that "ideal" which means a subset of an algebraic structure.

4

There are at least two ways of conceiving mathematics. One conceives it as something innate in the universe. Pythagoras held such conception. To him, numbers were divinities that made essence of all things and notions; he saw mathematical equations as the principle of the movements of planets and stars. Naturally, the use of such divinities for practical purposes was impious to him.

The founders of modern science such as Galileo, Kepler, Newton, were followers of Platonian mathematical cosmology. Plato was deeply influenced by Pythagoras in the view on mathematics and the universe. Those founders of modern science were thence Pythagorean.

To see how much influence those Greeks exerted upon them, it suffices to quote the following words from *Il Saggiatore* (*The Assayer*, 1623) written by Galileo:

> Philosophy is written in this grand book, the universe, which stands continually open to our gaze. But the book cannot be understood unless one first learns to comprehend the language and read the letters in which it is composed. It is written in the language of mathematics, and its characters are triangles, circles, and other geometric figures without which it is humanly impossible to understand a single word of it; without these, one wanders about in a dark labyrinth. (Drake, 4)

Galileo's word "philosophy" in the quotation above is synonym to science, for at that time, science and philosophy were one and the same.

Perhaps the most important in the quotation above is Galileo's assertion that science was "written in the language of mathematics" in the book named "the universe". This means that he conceived science not as a human invention but as a belonging of the universe, and that he was convinced that we could understand the universe only by way of mathematics. In other words, mathematics was a bridge between the universe and humans.

Another important point in the quotation is that mathematics was virtually geometry to him. That is why he referred to "triangles, circles, and other geometric figures". There was no room for algebra yet.

Now, the view on science and mathematics those founders of modern science held gave way to another one more familiar to us. According to this view that might be shared by many of us today, science and mathematics are human inventions and that we project them onto the universe. This view began to appear in the 18th century in Europe and spread over during the 19th. In the prologue of a book on history of mathematics, we find for example the following words:

> Mathematics is the oldest, deepest and purest discipline that human reason has created. (Nakamura/Muroi, iii)

In comparison with Pythagorean and Galilean conception, this one is much more anthropocentric.

But is the new vision truer than the old one? Roger Penrose (1959-), one of the most brilliant mathematicians and physicists of our days, asserted the following in his *The Large, the Small and the Human Mind* (1997):

> Some people (..) may prefer to think of mathematical concepts merely as idealizations of our physical world and on this view, the mathematical world would be thought of as emerging from the world of physical objects. Now, this is not how I think of mathematics, nor, I believe, is it how most mathematicians or mathematical physicists think about the world. They think about it (...) as a structure precisely governed according to timeless mathematical laws. Thus they prefer to think of the physical world (..) as emerging from the world of mathematics. (Penrose, No.155)

As we see, his position is clearly Platonian, for he believes that "the mathematical world" precedes "the physical world".

Now, which of the two conceptions above did our mathematician Oka hold? It is certain that he thought of mathematics as an academic discipline, an intellectual activity, but the fact that he compared a mathematician's life to the one of a violet in the wilderness as the following quotation shows implies that he thought of mathematics as emerging from Nature.

> People often ask me for what I am doing mathematics. For nothing, I answer them. I do mathematics just like violets that bloom out in a spring field. They bloom out without asking themselves for what they do it. There is difference between blooming and not blooming, for sure, but there is no reason for blooming or not. I study mathematics, I live on the joy it gives me, the joy of discovery, but that is not the aim. (Oka, 31)

He thought of mathematics as a human activity, but he saw that the activity came out of Nature. Nature creates mathematics in human mind just as She creates "violets" in spring fields. That was his view.

Now, the reference to violets in the quotation above reminds us of a poem of Basho (1644-94), the great master of haikai poetry he revered:

> Coming up on a mountain pathway   (Yamaji kite)
> Something is calling   (Naniyara yukashi)
> A violet!   (Sumire-gusa) (Basho, 63)

Together with the haikai master, Oka thought that he lived by Nature out of which mathematics was born to him.

His reference to "violets" also reminds us of Claude Lévi-Strauss' *La pensée sauvage* (1962). The title means "the savages' thought" or better to say, "human mind at its natural stage", but it also means "the wild violet" because "pensée" means "pansy", viola tricolor. The French anthropologist gave that name to his book seeing analogy between the wildflowers and the basic human thought.

5

Different from many mathematicians, Oka thought that mathematics came out of emotion, not of rationality. Let us read what he said on it:

> Mathematics is an academic art by which we draw our emotion on the canvas of intellect adapting ourselves to the form of what Western peoples call "mathematics". (Takase, ii)

To him, there was no intrinsic difference between art and mathematics; they were equally creations out of emotion.

This does not mean he considered them as totally the same. He said "They are both human creations, but mathematics has a scientific aspect that art does not have" (Takase, iii). He also said "The better half of mathematics is art. In my case, it is impossible to do mathematics without art." (Takase, 49).

Now, we cannot but wonder if mathematics could go without "reason". On this, we find the following words in his diary:

> When I discover something, I feel it beforehand. It is a warm feeling that invites me to go further. That feeling comes out of the uncertainty of discovery. If the discovery were certain, that warm feeling would not come up to me... It is therefore a question of feeling. But of course, I need reason that helps me distinguish one thing from another... Yes, I need reason as well. (Takase, 6-7)

He knew that "reason" was necessary for mathematical discovery to be realized, but its engine was "that warm feeling" of "uncertainty".

Now, is his word "feeling" the same as "emotion"? The original Japanese word he used for the former is "kan-jo" while the latter "jo-cho". He used them distinctly, and if we look carefully at the context in which he used them, we find that in his understanding, "feeling" was a specific and exterior form of "emotion" and this one was lying at the bottom of our mind. We may therefore say that he viewed mathematics as expression of the emotion at the bottom of our mind, and that doing mathematics made him have "that warm feeling" emerging on the surface of consciousness, urging him to discover something new.

In 1967, at the age of 66, Oka started to write essays for people who had no idea of mathematics. The main topic of them was the education of postwar Japan that he found "harmful" and "dangerous" because it neglected abovementioned "emotion" that he considered as the basis of human intelligence. In one of his first essays, he said:

> Many people believe that we realize our intellectual activities thanks to the brain cortex. But I would say it is our emotions that enable us to do it. (…) Emotions are related to our autonomous nerves. These nerves control our body including the brain. They are the center to our body and mind. They are the center to us humans. (Oka, 13)

He said this as warning to educators who did not have the slightest idea of the importance of emotion.

Now, his view on emotion is quite similar to Antonio Damasio's view. In *Descartes' Error* (1994), this world-famous brain scientist says the following based on empirical evidence:

> I propose that human reason depends on several brain systems, working in concert across many levels of neuronal organization, rather than on a single brain center. Both "high-level" and "low-level" brain regions...cooperate in the making of reason.
> The lower levels in the neural edifice of reason are the same ones that regulate the processing of emotions and feelings, along with the body functions necessary for an organism's survival. In turn, these lower levels maintain direct and mutual relationships with virtually

every bodily organ, thus placing the body directly within the chain of operations that generate the highest reaches of reasoning, decision making, and, by extension, social behavior and creativity. Emotion, feeling and biological regulation all play a role in human reason. (Damasio 1, xvii)

Damasio does not explain what "emotion" and "feeling" mean respectively there, but according to another book of his: *The Feeling of What Happens* (1999), the former is "patterns of response" coming out of the "basic life regulation" of the body to cope with changing environment, and that the feelings are "sensory patterns signaling pain, pleasure and other emotions by way of images". Those feelings, he adds, constitute our consciousness, and once consciousness is formed, we become conscious of our feelings, which enables us to develop "high reason" (Damasio 2, 55). This implies that we should develop children's emotion fully if we wish them to develop "high reason". Oka's view on education marvelously coincides with Damasio's neuroscientific view.

In the preface of the second edition of *Descartes' Error*, Damasio said that his stress on emotion was badly accepted by both specialists and non-specialists in the West (Damasio 1, ix-x). As for Oka's essays on the importance of emotion, they were much better accepted by his readers who were Japanese. This shows the difference as to the conception of emotion in the West and Japan. Damasio attacked Cartesian rationalistic culture dominant in the West; Oka warned the Japanese not to lose the basis of their cultural tradition.

Indeed, Oka insisted on emotion because he wanted his compatriots not to lose the tradition dear to him. He said:

Perhaps because Japanese culture has been centered on emotion, the Japanese capture the emotional basis of other cultures quickly. This characteristic is seen for example in Prince Shotoku's interpretations of Buddhist texts. It took him little time to seize the difficult texts of Buddhism because he captured the emotions behind them. (Oka, 39)

What he said about Japanese culture corresponds to what is said in the oldest book of Japanese history *Nihongi* (*Chronicle of Japan*, 720 A.D.) according to which Buddhism was accepted by the ancient Japanese not because of the depth of its philosophical theories but of the aesthetic emotion the images of Buddha evoked in them.

Now, the warning Oka made not to abandon the emotional basis of Japanese culture was not new in Japan. In the 18th century when rationalism was dominant in the intellectual society due to the influence of Neo-Confucianism introduced from China, Norinaga Motoori (1730-1801) insisted on emotional education by way of poetry. This one asserted that the basis of human mind was knowledge of the feelings that emerged as response to the influence of environment and that it was poetry that could teach the knowledge best (*Shibun Yo-ryo*, 1763). We can see that Oka's view and Moroori's are quite close to each other.

However, we should not overlook the difference lying between them. Motoori insisted on emotion without referring to any ideal because he conceived all emotions as manifestations of Divine Nature whereas Oka put stress on "ideal" as an important guide for emotion. The difference between the two is reflected on their religious tendency: Oka tended for Buddhism while Motoori for Shinto, a national religion based on reverence to Nature.

Although Oka cherished emotion, he saw its negative manifestations during the war. He could not accept all kinds of emotion as Motoori could have because he saw a series of irrational decisions and actions manifest in the wartime. To him, emotion had to be accompanied with an ideal which he distinguished from an ideology. In one of his essays, he said that the Japanese were an emotional and intuitive people, which was good itself, but they should discern what ideal to realize (Oka, 53).

Concerning his relation with Buddhism, we know that he studied the philosophy of Dogen (1200-53) after he came home from France. Dogen was a Buddhist monk of the 13th century who introduced Zen Buddhism from China to Japan.

After three years' stay in Paris, Oka began to study the poetry of Basho (1644-94) as well. Dogen and Basho became two masters to him. Basho, a great master of haikai poetry, was influenced by Zen Buddhism. If Oka said that the two were representatives of the genuine Japanese spirit, his "Japanese spirit" contained Buddhist "ideal".

One may wonder if Oka's notion of ideal did not have relevance to Platonism. For Plato was representative of idealism in the West and it was he who put stress on mathematics as the entrance to the world of ideals. In an essay titled "Joy of learning" (1962), Oka mentioned the name of Plato as a philosopher of the ideal. Let us have a look at the passage in which he mentioned the founder of Western philosophy:

> Although the Japanese capture other cultures quickly by way of emotions, they have difficulties in capturing Western culture, especially its Greek heritage. (…) There are two characteristics in the ancient Greek culture. On one hand, they estimated force and will too highly, which we should not introduce in our culture because such estimation of power is barbarian, having nothing to do with true culture. But they had on the other hand the independence of intellect which Japanese culture has hardly assimilated. We the Japanese will have to assimilate it by way of emotions because it is supremely important.

> The independence of intellect means complete freedom of thought that should never be disturbed or controlled by anything exterior to it. Only Greece gave such independence to intellect. Neither India nor China did it, which explains why there was no scientific development in Asia.

> It is often said that mathematics did not exist before Greece, which is correct because no mathematics elsewhere was so tenably structured as the Greek one. Mathematics was the bloom of intellect, and we should know that intellect was not the same as reason; it is

reason in quest of ideal. Indeed, it was the Greek who were the first to discover the notion of ideal and Plato's philosophy represented it. (Oka, 40)

Reading this, we see that Oka found a link between Dogen, Basho and Plato. Oka was a Buddhist, but he was also a mathematician who followed Plato's idealism.

6

We saw that Oka held a negative view on the mathematics of his time. He said it was like a "winter" scenery in which there was no life. However, the same Oka saw something positive in the same century as well, for he said that mathematics in the 20th century was returning to the original point at which the ideal of mathematics was born and that mathematicians began to observe Nature more carefully than ever (Oka, 44).

It is possible that he saw two extremes at the same time. He said that mathematical ideal was most beautifully manifest in the 19th century, especially in Bernhard Riemann's geometrical mathematics, and that the ideal was falling down in the 20th, but at the same time, he noticed that some mathematicians were becoming aware of it and began to recover the lost ideal by observing Nature as close as possible. He saw a hope in there.

I said earlier that his idealism was not very far from Platonian one, but he remained different from the Greek philosopher finding the ideal in our feeling, not in Nature or the universe. For he said:

In my view, the ideal of beauty, goodness, truth, does not belong to the world of reason but to our feeling of reality. In other words, we feel that it exits as real. (...) I think I am right because no one has ever shown us what it is, but many have spent the whole life seeking for it. (Oka, 43)

As we see, his position was always on human side, the side of those who feel. This seems to distinguish him from the Western intellectuals based on Plato's idealism.

Oka explained the ideal in the following manner:
> The ideal has such a power of attraction that makes us feel that we know a thing we have never seen. It resembles the feeling of a child looking for his mother he has never seen. The child can intuitively tell that a woman who is not his mother is not his mother even if he has never seen her. This indicates that the basic feeling of the ideal is longing. When the child says "She is not my mother", he says it intuitively, in other words, from the point of view of the ideal. (Oka, 43)

He translated the ideal to "longing". Let us remember that Plato associated the quest of the ideal to "reminiscence". Oka took the way of emotion to get to the ideal that Plato reached by way of memory, and Oka's "longing" has much to do with Plato's "reminiscence". Isn't this the same as "the feeling of a child looking for his mother he has never known"?

Oka sometimes referred to "mathematical nature" (*su-gaku-teki shizen*). What did he mean by it? As he was Platonian in his manner, we may assume that what he meant was something like ideal. Let us listen to his voice on it:
> There are two conditions for us to do mathematics. One is to find and raise up mathematical nature in our mind, and the other to open the intellectual eyes to watch that nature. To raise up mathematical nature in us, we must cultivate our emotions because our whole mental activities depend on them. It seems that the most appropriate age for a child to wake mathematical nature up in his mind is about 9 or 10. It is then that a child can feel the longing for the homeland of his mind; it is then that he can have the ideal as a vivid image.

(ibid. 44)

From this, we can see that to Oka, "mathematical nature" was the feeling of longing for the homeland of our mind we have never seen, in other words, the world of "ideal".

7

I already said that Oka began to read Basho and Dogen when he came home from France in 1932. Dogen was a Japanese Buddhist monk of the 13th century, and Basho, a master of haikai poetry of the 17th. Why did he choose those two out of many?

According to him, when he was in France, he felt something lacking there. After coming back to his homeland, he found what was lacking in the works of Dogen and Basho. We may imagine that he had a kind of home sick or suffered identity crisis during his stay in France, but even if so, that does not explain why he chose Dogen and Basho specifically; he could have chosen other thinkers or poets such as abovementioned Motoori, an influential representative of Japanese thought.

To find the true reason of the choice, we have to see the points common to Dogen and Basho. Dogen was a founder of Zen Buddhism in Japan, and Basho's poetry resulted from his practice of Zen meditations. Zen Buddhism born in China consists in a series of physical practice in accordance with a series of mental training. It aims at "Enlightenment" that consists in "no thinking". Dogen introduced it to Japan and spread it insisting that the meditation trainings had to be in accordance with the rhythm of the natural world. His aim was to establish perfect harmony between the body, the mind and Nature. Thus, he made a kind of synthesis of Shinto, the indigenous cult of Nature, and Buddhist philosophy that came from India through China. Oka must have been attracted by Dogen's worldview that he could not find in France.

He certainly saw mathematics highly developed in France, but he may have found disharmony between the intellectual life and Nature there. What he needed may therefore have been to find out the connecting point between mathematics and Nature. And we suppose that he found it in Dogen and Basho.

But how can we connect Dogen's Zen and mathematics? What is the connecting point of the two? I would say Zen connects with mathematics because it makes us aware of "function" between the body, the mind and the universe. It is a kind of mathematics, but without logic or numbers. Oka who was specializing in "theory of function" must have felt at home with Zen.

Another reason for his choice of Dogen can be explained in terms of the ideal. Oka may have found "the ideal" in the Zen master's view on Nature. In this one's masterpiece *Shobo Genzo* (*Treasury of the True Dharma Eye*, 1253?), we find the following words:

> Mountains and waters you are seeing now manifest the way and the words of the ancient Buddhas. Staying in the right position under the Laws, they make infinite grace to you. As they are beyond time and space, they are living here and now. As their self is beyond time and eternity, they are here free from their selves. (…) Let us remember Master Kwai once said to his disciples "Blue mountains never cease walking; barren women give birth to babies during the night." Mountains always stay stable and walk on because there is nothing they can't. Mountains walk just like us, which you should not doubt even if you don't see it. (Dogen, 53-54)

"Mountains and waters" Dogen referred to were not natural entities but messengers of Buddha's "ideal". He invited us to read Buddha's words written in Nature. Let us remember that Galileo invited us to read the text of science carved in the universe (*Il Saggiatore*, 1623). Isn't there something very similar between the two?

It is certain Galileo and his followers took the way of mathematics while Dogen the way of Zen meditation and physical trainings. Oka was a mathematician, but he must have found Dogen's way more complete than mathematics. Dogen may have looked to him like a more complete mathematician than all the mathematicians he knew.

Dogen's words quoted above imply that to understand Buddha's teachings, we should observe and understand Nature. It is not enough to receive and enjoy the gift *She* gives us; we must walk in accordance with *Her* movements. To walk means to make bodily movements instead of intellectual movements. It must be this philosophy that Oka felt lacking in France.

Now, as for Oka's keen interest in Basho, the haikai master, he must have found the same inquiry of ideal in the poet as in Dogen. Basho was an idealist in his manner as the following quotation from his essay *Oi-no Kobumi* (*Small writings in a Box on My Back* 1688) shows:

> There is only one truth in art and poetry. We find it in Saigyo's waka poetry, Sogi's renga poetry, Sesshu's drawings and Rikyu's art of tea ceremony. All the beautiful is in concordance with changing Nature, having friendship with four seasons. Everything you see is a splendid flower; everything you have in mind is a sublime moon. If you don't see it, you are a barbarian. If your mind is not a flower, you are a beast. Let's abandon the barbarians and the beasts in us to go back to Nature and obey Her. (Basho 2, 52)

"All the beautiful is in concordance with changing Nature, having friendship with four seasons." That is the phrase by which Basho expressed his ideal. Let us remember Oka once said that mathematics of his time had become "winter" and he wanted it to turn to "spring". He sought for "the beautiful" in mathematics in "concordance with changing Nature, having friendship with four seasons."

We wonder now how the names of Dogen and Basho came up to his mind. Had he known them before going to France? I would rather say "no" because there is no mention of either of them in his writings about his childhood or school days. He was interested in and fond of mathematics, but not of religion or philosophy or literature then.

So far as Basho is concerned, he may have learned about the poet when he was in Paris, for he had good friends there: Ukichiro Nakaya (1900-62), a physicist from Japan, and Jyujiro (1902-36), his younger brother who was an archeologist. They were both quite familiar with haikai poetry. Oka enjoyed exchanging ideas with them on science and other topics including haikai poetry.

Nakaya brothers were both followers of Torahiko Terada (1878-1935) who was a physicist and a haikai poet. Their knowledge and practice of haikai poetry must have come from it. On the souvenir of his encounter with them in Paris, Oka said longingly:

> The best thing I got in France was the acquaintance of Jyujiro Nakaya, Ukichiro's brother. He was a young archeologist who came to France on his own, by way of Siberia. He had just written a long article about Jo-mon pottery he collected here and there in Tohoku region in Japan. He gave me its abstract in French in which I found a talent. As he was young, he did not know his strength or weakness yet, but I was struck by his brilliance and knowledgeability. What was appreciable in him was the high ideal he held for his studies. I was so happy talking with him. Once he showed me his ideal in form of haikai poetry. It read "opening the door, not fully, just enough to let see the flowers inside." (Oka, 29)

The best way of communication among them were that kind of exchanging haikai poems.

As for Dogen, we are not sure if they talked on this one in Paris. It seems probable that Oka discovered Basho first and Dogen later. For he said the following in an essay titled "Becoming aware of Japanese mind" (1966):

> From 1929 till 32, I was in Paris. I found there something very important lacking. I started then to find out what was lacking, which led me to study the essential of Japanese culture. I studied Basho and his haikai poetry (…) which led me to discover the emotional basis of Japanese culture.
>
> Each culture, each nation, has its own color of emotions. Basho represents the color of Japanese emotion. In other words, the color of his personal emotions perfectly corresponds to the one of the Japanese. (…) However, Basho was not sufficient for me to assimilate Japanese mind. I needed someone else and saw that Zen master Dogen was the right one. Thanks to his books, I could finally draw the image of Japanese mind. (Oka, 291-292)

We see that to find out the essential of his traditional culture, Oka read Basho first, and then Dogen came up to show him the philosophical basis of Basho.

I would like to insist here that what he meant by "Japanese mind" was not a nationalistic ideology, but rather the ideal of Japanese tradition. For he said "If a person whose personal color of emotion corresponds to the color of the traditional emotion of the Japanese, I will call him a pure Japanese. Thence, many who believe to be Japanese are not Japanese while foreigners who have the emotional color of Japanese tradition are genuine Japanese even if they are officially not Japanese" (Oka, 292). This shows that being Japanese was not the question of nationality or race to him but the question of spirit, attitude, the ideal.

Oka thought of Basho and Dogen representatives of the ideal of Japanese mind. Do today's Japanese agree with him in the regard? They would not be able to answer the question because, I dare say, there is no more ideal in today's Japanese mind. With the accelerated modernization of the country, they have lost their spiritual basis. To fill the void they feel, they either cling to political ideologies such as nationalism, capitalism, socialism, etc., or tired of ideologies, indulge themselves in material comforts.

In 1936, four years after his return to Japan, Jyujiro Nakaya, Oka's best friend, died of tuberculosis. Longing for him, Oka wrote the following:

> What I gained during my stay abroad were two. First, by leaving Japan, I could transcend time and space. Secondly, I knew true friendship by the encounter with Jyujiro. I was supposed to pass two years in Paris, but I asked the authorities to extend it up to three years because I wanted to have more time with him. We came back to Japan together in 1932, but soon after, he went to a spa in Kyushu to stay there for a long time to be cured of the spinal cord caries he had. During each summer vacation, I went there to visit him, but the third visit was the last one. I learned later that he made a haikai poem just after my last visit. The poem reads: "Crossing the hills, hearing the sirens, departure". I realize now that so long as he was there to talk with me, I didn't feel the need to study mathematics. When he passed away in March 1936, I finally allowed myself to be absorbed in mathematics. (Oka, 29-30)

After Jyujiro's death, Oka kept friendship with his brother Ukichiro who helped him in many ways. Oka said that Ukichiro was a "practical" man while this one who was a specialist in snow crystals saw a sociopath genius in Oka. He not only helped him find a job when this one was dismissed by the university he worked for, but also gave him private lessons on physics at home.

Their beautiful friendship can be seen in the following exchange of haikai poetry:

Ukichiro: Early autumn, alive in the water tub, remains of blossoms
Oka: The light of sunset filtering, the sound of the water removed
Ukichiro: Autumn sea, to cloudless sky, continues
Oka: Without any footprint, a morning on the white sand

(Oka, 46)

Regrettably, todays' Japanese have no more practice of this kind of communication. Maybe there are some who realize it by sending text messages on a mobile phone.

On the haikai verses quoted above, I have to add that they made it just to measure how many seconds they needed to make it. It took only "10 seconds". Oka compared this with the time the school children of postwar Japan needed to answer a very simple logical question and found that they needed "270,000 seconds" for it. He was shocked at the difference and said in a warning tone that it was because the children were educated to say "yes" to everything whether they understood it or not (Oka, 46). He saw disaster in Japanese postwar education.

Oka's warning may apply to today's Japanese school education as well. "To say yes to everything without understanding it" continues.

To end this article, I would like to quote a passage from his essay titled "Japanese emotion" (1963). It exactly shows what ideal he wished to realize by his mathematics:

> When I was a college student, I discussed with a classmate during lunch time. I remember that I finally said to him "I will do mathematics without computation, without logic." Someone who happened to hear me cried out "Aren't you joking, Mr. Oka?" Then I found myself surprised by my own words. (…) Many years have passed since then, and I can say with conviction that computation and logic are both illusions. When I am absorbed in mathematics, I have no time to think of logic or computation because if I think of it, I will have to stop the stream of my consciousness, which is fatal to mathematics. Computation and logic do not make anything essential to mathematics. (Oka, 70)

Did Oka realize mathematics "without computation, without logic"? I have not enough knowledge of mathematics to answer it. But I can see that his ideal of mathematics was no different from poetry.

Works Cited

Basho 1: *Basho Ku-shu (Anthology of Hokku)*, Tokyo, Iwanami Publishing, 1985

Basho 2 : *Basho Bun-shu (Anthology of Proses)*, Tokyo, Iwanami Publishing, 1970

Damasio, Antonio 1: *Descartes' Error, Emotion, Reason, and the Human Brain*, New York, Penguin Books, 1994

Damasio, Antonio 2 : *The Feeling of What Happens*, London, Vintage, 2000

Dogen : *Shobo Genzo vol.2 (Treasury of the True Dharma Eye)*, Tokyo, Sei-shin Shobo, 1972

Drake, Stillman : *Discoveries and Opinions of Galileo* (New York, Doubleday & Co., 1957) in https://web.stanford.edu/~jsabol/certainty/readings/Galileo-Assayer.pdf

Nakamura, S./Muroi, K : *Su-gaku-shi (History of Mathematics)*, Tokyo, Kyo-ritsu Publishing, 2015

Oka, Kiyoshi : *Oka Kiyoshi-shu Vol.1 (Collected Works 1)*, Tokyo, Gakken Publishing, 1969

Penrose, Roger : *The Large, the Small and the Human Mind* (Cambridge, Cambridge University Press, 1999) in Canto edition (2000)

Poincaré, Henri : *La valeur de la science* (*The Value of Science*, Paris, Flammarion, 1911) in https://fr.wikisource.org/wiki/La_Valeur_de_la_Science

Takase, Masahito : *Oka Kiyoshi - Su-gaku no Shijin - (Kiyoshi Oka, a Mathematical Poet)*, Tokyo, Iwanami Publishing, 2008

Chapter 5

Poetry, Religion and Science in Kenji Miyazawa

1

Kenji Miyazawa (1896-1933) was completely unknown during his lifetime. But today, he is considered as one of the most original poets and the best story tellers for children in Japan. In his poems and stories, we find an unusually beautiful mixture of science and religion, the natural and the artificial, the archaic and the ultramodern. His language is original, sometimes difficult to understand, yet magically attractive.

He is known to be a poet, but he did not consider himself as such. The following is a quotation from a letter he wrote to a friend Saichi Mori on February 9 in 1925:

> As you know, I published a book titled Spring and Ashura for myself. People thought it is a poetic anthology. (…) But all the words you find there are not "poems" at all. They are simply rough sketches of the images coming up to my mind under different circumstances, the images that I keep in words for a future investigation of psychology to which I cannot dedicate much time for the moment. (Miyazawa, vol. 9, 281)

As we see, what we consider as his poems were nothing more than data for his psychological studies to come.

We find the same assertion in the letter he addressed to Shigeo Iwanami, the founder and president of Iwanami Publishers, one of the most influential in Japan of his time. The letter was written on December 20 in 1925:

> For the last 6 or 7 years, I have been wondering if the current notions of history, its data, space and time are correct. Those notions hardly convince me. As I am a teacher at an agronomical school in the north-east region, having unfortunately no time for philosophical studies, I have dedicated my time to record different stages of my mind in a scientific way, without any modification, in case that they could be useful for my future studies. (Miyazawa, vol.9, 298-299)

Although he did not mention the word "psychology" there, he declared that his "poems" were not poems but scientific, high-fidelity records of "different stages" of his mind.

Now, he mentioned the "philosophical studies" in the letter. As he referred to the "current notions of history, its data, space and time", we understand that he meant a new philosophical standpoint from which he could review them. He felt a need to review the basic notions of modern science and history to open up a new philosophical horizon.

Returning to his notion of poetry, we cannot but wonder if he really thought that his poems were not poems. For in the letter to Shigeo Iwanami quoted above, we find the following words as well:

> I would not say I ignore poetry, but I was not happy to see people taking the high-fidelity records of my mind for valueless patchworks. (Miyazawa, vol.9, 299)

What he meant is that he would not accept people to take his psychological records for "poetry" because in his conception, poetry was nothing more than ensemble of "valueless patchworks". This indicates that he had a very low estimation of poetry.

If he considered poetry as such, it is because most of the poems he knew must have been composed of elements coming from different poetical sources, nothing more. To him, poetry had to be otherwise, more original, more creative.

Now, if he did not consider his poems as "poems", Kenji considered his stories for children as literary works. In the advertising text for his book *Chumon no Ooi Ryori-ten* (*Restaurant with too many orders*,1924), he said as follows:

> Everything is possible in this world of fantasy. We can fly to the cold clouds within an instant and travel to the North Pole accompanied by the winds; we can also talk with ants walking beneath the red flower cups. Sins, errors, even sorrows, are shining pure here. (…)
> This series of stories for children are descriptions of some images that came up to the author's mind. They are presented in a literary form apt for those who are ending their childhood or entering in the mid-adolescence. (Miyazawa K, 3-12/82)

There he clearly said that his stories for children and adolescents were literary works even if they were based on the images coming up to his mind the high-fidelity records of which he did not recognize as literature.

2

Let us examine Kenji's ideal of poetry. The story titled "Ryu to Shijin" (The Dragon and the Poet, 1921) helps us see it. It begins with the following words:

> Chahnata the Dragon tried to get his body out of the cave filled with the flowing tides. The shining morning sun lighted up the silhouette of the rock at the bottom of the water in the cave together with the

red and white animals on it. Chahnata looked at the blue water, half dreaming. (…)

"I could swim freely through the oceans of all the planet, I could fly over the pure air as far as I could. But alas, I can't get out of this cave. All I can do is to have a glimpse of the universe from here just through the narrow hole." Thus, he lamented, looking back to the inside of the cave. Then, suddenly, he heard a voice of someone young saying "Oh, Divine King of Dragon, Divine King Dragon, I beg you to pardon me and wipe me off the error I committed." He looked out and heard again the same voice saying "Old Chahnata, I have come here, thanks to the morning sun power, to beg your pardon humbly." Finally, he saw a youngster with ornaments and a golden sword, seated on a paving stone with green moss.

(Miyazawa, vol.6, 61-62)

The youngster was named Surdahta; he came to see Chahnata the Dragon to beg pardon for the error he thought he had committed. He won a prize in a poetry competition, but he thought that he had stolen a part of the Dragon's song to compose his. However, Chahnata the Dragon did not punish him because he conceived poetical creation differently. He explained his conception, saying the following:

Oh, Surdahta, the song I sang and you heard out of which you think you stole something is yours as well as mine. Besides, I am still uncertain if I sang it or just thought of it. Did you hear my song coming near my cave or just think of it? Anyway, don't you see that I was clouds and winds at that moment? Don't you see that you were also clouds and winds? Other poets could have sung the same if they had meditated at that moment sitting around here. Their words are not the same as yours, and yours are not the same as mine, nor are the rhymes. Your song is yours and it came out of the same spirit as mine that shares the power of the clouds and the winds.

(Miyazawa, vol.6, 63-64)

In short, according to the Dragon, poetical creation does not belong to anyone particular but to "the clouds and the winds". He regarded them as the only source of inspiration out of which each poet could compose a poem in his or her language. With this idea, the Dragon naturally did not punish Surdahta, the young poet. So long as they are inspired by the same clouds and winds, poets have no possibility of stealing or borrowing poems from others. That was the Dragon's conception of poetical creation.

Kenji's ideal of poetry was right there. Like Chahnata the Dragon, he believed in the inspiration by the "clouds and winds" out of which poets could compose a song, each one in his or her language.

Now, this conception of the clouds and winds as the source of poetical inspiration reminds us of the idea of poetical creation held by Arthur Rimbaud (1854-91). In the letter to Paul Demeny on May 15 in 1871, the young French poet said the following:

> I is another one. If copper wakes up as a trumpet, it is not its fault at all. To me, it is so obvious: I observe the eclosion of my thought, watch it, listen to it, and throw an arrow onto it. Then, the symphony begins to move in the depth or comes out on the scene abruptly. (Rimbaud, 315)

As the quotation shows, Rimbaud conceived poetical creation as a phenomenon beyond himself as if it had happened to someone else. He did not use the words such as "winds" or "clouds", but "human intelligence" just to express the same idea as Kenji. In the same letter to Demeny, we find the following words:

> Human intelligence has always thrown its ideas; and people have harvested a part of its fruit produced by the brains. (Rimbaud, 315-316)

Of course, "human intelligence" is not exactly the same as "clouds and winds". Rimbaud was more humanist than Kenji, we might say, or Kenji was more naturalist than Rimbaud. However, their views were not so different as they appear. For what the French poet called "human intelligence" each human brain might capture is not in us but in the air just like what we call "cloud computing system" today.

Now, "clouds and winds" Kenji considered as source of poetic inspiration belong to Nature. We have to put stress on it to distinguish it from the abovementioned "cloud computing system" that is artificial. Indeed, his inspiration source was in Nature. The following words in the advertising text for his book mentioned above show it:

> These stories are fresh products of the fields and gardens. The author has decided to offer the sketches of his mental images, the winds and lights of the fields and gardens to the world, together with elegant fruits and green vegetables. (Miyazawa K, 22/82)

His thought that true inspiration has to come from Nature or direct contact with Nature is manifest for example in his story titled "Sero hiki no Goshu" (Gauche, the violoncello player, 1934). This is a story that tells that true inspiration, whether in music or not, comes from Nature.

The story is of a young man named Gauche who is a member of an orchestra. He plays the violoncello so unskillfully that one day, the conductor scolds him severely at the rehearsal. Discouraged, he comes home, but recovers courage by drinking a lot of water, and soon begins to train himself on the play. He plays it all through the night and this continues for several nights. Now, every night he trains himself, different animals come up to ask him to play something for them. He is reluctant to do it, but each time he does it, he sees improvement in his performance. One early morning, a cuckoo comes up to ask him to play the "cuckoo's do-re-mi", which he finds too difficult. However, he makes efforts to play it and finally manages it. From that experience, he learns the importance of going back to the very natural stage of music. Since then, he is another person, another spirit, another musician whose performance is amazingly touching to the audience. At the concert, he is a shining star of the orchestra. The lesson of this happy ending story is easy to catch: we should listen to the music of Nature if we want to play music well.

3

In 1926, Kenji opened the night school for the farm workers living near him so that these could learn music, drawings as well as basic agronomy. He especially put stress on artistic activities, finding them indispensable for them to live with joy. The idea of the school is manifest in his "Nomin Geijutsu Gairon Koryo" (Manifesto for the Farming People's Art, 1926). The quotation below is a part of the manifesto:

Why is the farm workers' art necessary?

Just remember that our ancestors used to live happily despite poverty.

They had art and religion.

Today, we have only labor to survive.

Religion is tired, replaced by science, and science is cold and dark.

As for art, it has gone far away from us and finds itself miserably degenerated.

Those who are called religious people or artists today are nothing more than merchants who monopolize truth, good or beauty.

We have no money to buy them, but we do not need them, either.

We have to go straight on the new and righteous way to create beauty that is ours.

We have to fire the grey labor red with art!

Thus we can enjoy our incessant and pure creation.

City people, come and join us!

World, accept our wish that has nothing wrong!

(Miyazawa, vol.11, 11)

Kenji saw that there was only art that could help the workers live on with joy because they had no more religion that could have given them warmth and light. The only hope he found was in art.

Now, the art he was thinking of was not the one conceived by the people of his time. He regarded the art of his days as "miserably degenerated" because of its commercialization. He found it necessary to create a new one that could make the workers happier.

His idea of the new art for the workers reminds us of the thought of Simone Weil (1909-43), a French philosopher contemporary to him. Working in automobile factories, she discovered that the factory workers needed poetry above everything else. In "Condition première d'un travail non servile" (1941), she said:

> People need poetry like bread. Not poetry enclosed in words that cannot be of any use to them. They need the substance of their everyday life to be poetry. (Weil 1, 219)

Although she did not indicate the way to make the "substance" of the workers' life "poetry", she saw the same lack in the modern workers' life as Kenji. They both saw in them lack of religion, spirituality, poetry, joy.

Now, in *La pesanteur et la grace* (1947), her posthumous work, Weil said what kind of poetry the workers needed:

> Workers need poetry more than bread. They need their life to be a poetry, light of eternity. Only religion can be the source of the poetry they need. The opium for people is not religion but revolution. If they are demoralized in a way or another, it is because they are deprived of that poetry. (Weil 2, 204)

There she affirmed that the poetry the workers needed was a spiritual one that she called "light of eternity". That poetry had to come out of "religion". As for Kenji, he expressed almost the same idea, but of course, in different words. In the abovementioned manifesto, he said the following:

> The farm people's art aims at beauty, of course.
> But the beauty we need is no more the same beauty as has been conceived; aesthetics changes incessantly.

The new beauty will spread to the infinite till the word "beauty" disappears.

We have to be alert not to choose the wrong way, not to fall into a trap.

The farm people's art must be concrete expression of the cosmic emotion and the expression must be accessible to Earth, people and individuals.

It must be conscious or unconscious creation out of intuition and emotion inside us.

It must affirm our everyday life, elevate it and deepen it.

It must be incessant motion pictures or inexhaustible poetry of our life and Nature.

It must teach us to appreciate and enjoy our life and Nature like cosmic dances and theaters.

It must make our spirit communicate with others' and socialize the common feeling up to the universal.

Thus, it will form the very basis of our new culture.

(Miyazawa, vol. 11, 12)

What he called "cosmic emotion" does not seem to be far from Weil's "light of eternity". It was something transcendent and immanent to us.

4

We saw that Kenji found science "cold and dark". But this does not mean that he hated science. On the contrary, he was very fond of it and studied it hard. He found it necessary to our life.

Indeed, we do not find in him any hatred of science typical to the Romantics such as John Keats (1795-1821). This one expressed it in the poem titled Lamia (1819) as follows:

Do not all charms fly

At the mere touch of cold philosophy?
There was an awful rainbow once in heaven:
We know her woof, her texture; she is given
In the dull catalogue of common things.
Philosophy will clip an Angel's wings,
Conquer all mysteries by rule and line,
Empty the haunted air, and gnomed mine—
Unweave a rainbow, as it erewhile made
The tender-person'd Lamia melt into a shade.

Keats hated science because he thought that it deprived Nature of "all charms" and "mysteries". Science put "rainbow", he said, into "the dull catalogue of common things" by "unweaving" it. To him, science was just "cold and dark".

Kenji who found science "cold and dark" had another conception of it. He held a hope that science might be compatible with religion and art. For in the manifesto mentioned above, he said:

> From the unified perspective of modern positive science, ancient religious experiments and our intuition, we can assert that there is no individual happiness so long as happiness of the whole universe is not achieved. (Miyazawa 11, 10)

He saw the possibility of unification of science, art and religion.

He was always amazed at the beauty and the mystery of Nature, but different from Keats, he found science helpful for him to approach the secrets of Nature. In this, he had the same scientific spirit that Richard Dawkins (1941-), a biologist of our days, holds. This one sees no difference between scientists and poets because he finds in both the same "sense of wonder" before Nature.

Kenji did not hate science for a practical reason as well. He found science useful and efficient to improve people's life at least on the material level.

He appreciated for example medical science able to cure diseases. He went to Morioka School of Agronomy in order to make the farming people's life easier with the scientific knowledge of agriculture that he would acquire there. He had seen many disasters falling upon people because of bad weather, earthquakes, tsunamis. He hoped to lessen their suffering using scientific knowledge.

At Morioka School of Agronomy, he learned biology, geology, chemistry, meteorology and agronomy to become an agricultural engineer. As he was fond of stars and planets, he also taught himself astronomy, physics and mathematics after school. According to Michiko Ryo, there remain 50 books on science in his collection among which 17 are on mathematics, 12 on geology and mineralogy, 9 on chemistry, 9 on agronomy and gardening, 2 on physics, 1 on engineering (Ryo, 2005).

He also possessed Japanese version of the collection *The Outline of Science* (1922) edited by J. Arthur Thomson. This collection included biology, astronomy, physics, psychology, even spiritualism. By reading all those, Kenji composed the poetically scientific vision of the universe that we find in his poems and stories. If his notion of science included psychology and spiritualism, it is surely due to the influence of J.A. Thomson's collection.

In fact, among the sciences Kenji studied, psychology occupied a special place in him. As he did not have a chance to learn it at the agronomy school, he learned it for himself through the Western books translated into Japanese. We know he took much interest in William James' works, especially in this one's descriptions of consciousness. The fact he was eager to describe the mental images that came to his mind and record them for future psychological studies proves it.

5

I said above that Kenji found science useful and efficient to improve people's life. One of the examples that show the pragmatic side of his thought on modern science is found in the story he wrote for children, titled *Gusko Budori no Denki* (*The Life of Budori Gusuko*, 1932). It is a story of a young engineer named Budori. Here is the outline:

Budori lost his parents when he was a child because of the famine caused by cool summer. He lost his sister at the same time, and did not know if she was still alive. He found a job in a factory, but it was soon shut down because of the eruption of a volcano nearby. He became a farm worker then, but it was terribly hard to work on sterile lands.

What saved him out of the misery was the encounter with a great scientist, Doctor Koobo. The doctor, finding the boy intelligent and diligent, adopted him as an assistant and taught him sciences necessary for him to become an engineer to cope with volcanic activities. His life drastically changed then.

Once he assimilated the basic knowledge of sciences, he began to work at the disaster prevention station as an engineer and succeeded in diminishing the volcanic damages and irrigating the sterile lands by artificial rainfalls. He became happy with all this.

He was also happy because he finally met his sister of whom he had had no news for a long time. She was married and looked happy.

However, another cool summer came menacing the whole region with great famine. To see it, Budori thought of making an artificial volcano eruption so that the carbon dioxide gas coming out of it could warm the soil with its greenhouse effect. On hearing this project, Dr. Koobo said it was a good idea but difficult to realize without having a victim. For there would have to be someone who would stay near the volcano to provoke the eruption. Budori did not hesitate to propose that himself would be the one who would provoke the eruption. Against the disagreement of the doctor and other colleague engineers, he did it unhesitant, and died once he saw the experiment successful. The whole region was saved from famine. (Miyazawa vol.10)

The story is happy ending though the hero dies. There are many who consider it as a story of beautiful self-sacrifice. As for its scientific aspect, we cannot but question the optimistic view the author presented there. Indeed, it is too optimistic.

We know there was such optimism concerning science and technology prevalent in Japan before World War II. Japanese intellectuals tended to think of science as indispensable means for the national survival in the international society without questioning or examining its philosophical basis. They hardly thought of the possibility that it could do harm to people. Kenji was not an exception.

In the case of his hero Budori, who made an artificial eruption of a volcano which saved the local people from cold summer, if he had not made it successfully, the damage could have been huge to them. Even if he had made it successfully, his experiment could have caused problems to environment that he might not have foreseen. As I said above, Kenji was too optimistic as to science and its applications.

If he had seen the A-bombs' tremendous effects, if he had known the atrocious human body experiments some scientists of his country realized during the war, would Kenji still have had the same optimism? Many people still hold the idea that science itself is neutral and that it can be good or bad depending on the aim of its application, but the pretended neutrality is questionable. Scientists must know that they are responsible for the problems their researches can bring about.

6

I said earlier that Kenji saw the possibility of unification of science, art and religion. This means science was an indispensable element of his worldview. As a matter of fact, he tried to see the world from a scientific perspective although he never thought of this as the only valid one. He had a complex viewpoint from which he regarded everything.

> The phenomenon called I
> is a blue lighting of hypothetical organic alternate electric current
> (a complex of all kinds of transparent ghosts)
> (Miyazawa, vol. 2, 3)

The three lines above is the very beginning part of the prologue of his anthology titled *Haru to Shura* (*Spring and Asura*, 1924). Analyzing these, we can see how complex his worldview was.

The first line "The phenomenon called I" sounds Buddhist, for one of the Buddhists principles is "There is nothing substantial but only phenomena". As a matter of fact, Kenji was a passionate Buddhist so that we may associate the phrase to Buddhism.

However, the term "phenomenon" itself (*gensho* in Japanese) is a philosophical and scientific term coming from the West. The fact he used it shows his openness to science and Western philosophy.

The second line "a blue lighting of hypothetical organic alternate electric current" sounds scientific. It says that the phenomenon called *I* is an electric lighting and that the electric current that makes it is "organic" and "alternate". This leads us to suppose that Kenji had the scientific knowledge that some elements in an organic body such as sodium, potassium, calcium, magnesium, have electric charge.

However, the electricity in our body does not necessarily make "lighting", nor a "blue" one as he said. Did Kenji create an image of a human being by mixing his scientific knowledge and fantasy? Or he just described what he perceived? We will see the answer to the questions a bit later.

As for the word "hypothetical", it indicates that he was aware of the hypothetical nature of his theory of I. He must have known that he had no evidence to prove it. And let us remember that "hypothetical" is another scientific term introduced from the West to Japan. Kenji must have known that science consists in establishing hypothesis and proving their veracity empirically.

The third line put in parenthesis is a presentation of a different version of the theory put forward above. For we know that when Kenji used parenthesis, it is often when he wanted to add another version of the thought he had already expressed. "A complex of all kinds of transparent ghosts" is then another version or another definition of the "phenomenon called I". He saw his I as "a complex of all kinds of transparent ghosts".

Now, this implies that he believed in the ghosts and the spirits of the dead. How could it be so if he trusted science? We know that most scientists are materialists who deny the existence of ghosts, and many people of our time follow them. However, there were and still are some scientists called spiritualists who believe in it. Kenji was one of them.

He must have read Oliver Lodge's article on his communication with his lost son Raymond (Lodge, 1916). Lodge was a first-rate physicist, and his article on his son was contained in Japanese version of *The Outline of Science* edited by J. Arthur Thomson (1922) he possessed. He must have felt deep sympathy with the author of the article. For he had lost his beloved sister Toshi two years earlier than the publication of the anthology *Spring and Asura*.

In one of his poems collected in the anthology, we find the following stanza:

Oh, Toshi, My Toshi
I can't help remembering you
When I come to a wide field
When I stand in the wind
Are you above that gigantic Jupiter
Beyond the splendid steely blue sky?
But I can't but wonder if there really are in that invisible space
Strings of light and its orchestra
   … Here the day is long, infinitely long
   I can't tell what time it is….
Just one piece of your voice, nothing more,
Reached me when I was in the train
But I don't know exactly when (June 3, 1923)
(Miyazawa, vol. 2, 156)

He heard the voice of his dead sister coming from the unknown "space" that he thought to be beyond "the gigantic Jupiter". Although he held belief in science, his personal experiences taught him that there were ghosts.

I said earlier that the three first lines of the prologue of his anthology present the very structure of Kenji's complex vision of the universe. After having examining them, we can safely say that it is composed of science on one side, spiritualism on the other, and Buddhism that covers all.

As for the "blue lighting" in the second line, we see that it came out of his spiritualistic view. For the blue lighting is what we associate with a ghost at least in Japan whether it is scientifically justifiable or not.

7

In the same prologue of the anthology we have been examining, we find surprising views of the universe such as this one:

Humans, galaxies, asuras, sea urchins
Eating cosmic dusts, drinking air or salty water
Each one of them may invent a different ontology
But all those are after all nothing more than different mental sceneries (Miyazawa, vol. 2, 4)

The order of the terms: "humans", "galaxies", "asuras" "sea urchins", may look strange, but the quotation shows that Kenji viewed all of them as living beings, recognizing each one having its own "ontology", *hontai-ron* in Japanese. He understood the term "ontology" as a story of reality that each one constructs. To him, there was no reality but "mental sceneries", in other words, consciousness. In this, he was loyal to Buddhist theory of consciousness according to which reality is nothing but an illusory construct.

Kenji was indeed a dedicated Buddhist to whom everything in the world had consciousness. That is why he asserted that "humans, galaxies, asuras, sea urchins" had their own ontologies, each one making a different one.

The fact he used the term "*asuras*" is another proof of his being Buddhist. *Asura* is a Buddhist term that means a figting spirit with human weaknesses. He found himself as an asura split between the human and the angelic, the earthly and the heavenly. We understand why the title of the anthology is *Spring and Asura*.

The last words of the quotation above: "mental sceneries", leave us with a question. "Mental sceneries" of whom? Apparently, Kenji's, but he did not say "my mental sceneries". The following quotation from "Manifesto for the Art of the Farm Workers" may supply an answer for it:

Our consciousness gradually evolves from our individual self to a collective one, from a collective one to the one of the whole universe. (Miyazawa 11, 10)

If "consciousness" evolves from an individual one to a collective one, from a collective one to a cosmic one as he said, "mental sceneries" could not belong to anyone but to the very process of evolution of consciousness. In other words, the everchanging universe has consciousness and that all the consciousnesses, individual or social, human or animal, are different stages of its evolution.

Kenji knew quite well that people believed to have consciousness of their own, but their consciousness was not connected to the universal consciousness. He believed that lack in connection with the universal consciousness was the very cause of their unhappiness. Himself inquired after it by way of science, art and religion. And it was Lotus Sutra, one of the Buddhist texts, that gave the final answer to him. That is why he became an ardent believer in the sutra. The words such as "I am everyone's self and everyone's self is mine" that we find in the prologue of *Spring and Asura* are the expression of the higher stage of consciousness he attained with the help of the sutra.

Now, his approach being Buddhist, one may regard him as a religious man, but this does not mean that he abandoned science. Till the end of his life, he kept studying his mind scientifically in order to find the objective foundation for what he had discovered by way of Buddhism. He sought for the unification point of science and religion.

Many would argue against him asserting that there cannot be any objective foundation for the "universal consciousness". But if there is no evidence for such consciousness to exist, there is no evidence to prove the contrary, either. Let us listen to quantum physicists such as Roger Penrose (1931-) who are trying to find out the physical basis for consciousness in the universe (Consciousness and the Universe, 2009).

We can never say that Kenji was mistaken.

At the end of the prologue of *Spring and Asura*, Kenji referred to the "fourth dimension". He said that all the propositions he put forward in the prologue were mental images that were only "real" in the fourth dimension (Miyazawa 2, 6). We do not know how much he knew of Relativity Theory, but what is interesting is that he found Einstein's theory of time-space more real than other theories. It seems that he saw a connection between his "universal consciousness" and Einstein's theory.

8

As we saw earlier in the letter he addressed to Shigeo Iwanami, Kenji did not believe in the modern notion of time or space:

> For the last 6 or 7 years, I have been wondering if the current notions of history, its data, space and time that we perceive, are correct. (Miyazawa 9, 298)

His mistrust on those notions of modernity seems to have been reinforced by Einstein's time-space notion. From his spiritualist viewpoint, he seems to have found affinity with Relativity Theory.

But physics was not the only science that encouraged him. He obtained a totally different view on time, space and history, thanks to his knowledge of astronomy, geology and biology. The following quotation from the prologue of his anthology is one of the examples that show his knowledge of such sciences:

> However, these words that must have been copied without fault
> During the hugely illuminated accumulation of time
> Of Alluvium in Cenozoic Era
> Have already lost their structure and quality
> Within a blink equivalent to a tiniest point in the universe

(Or Asura's billion years)
And yet I and my printer possibly tend to feel
That they have not changed at all. (Miyazawa 2, 5)

Referring to his words collected in the anthology, he said that written in "Alluvium in Cenozoic Era", they were losing its structure and quality within a blink equivalent to "a tiniest point in the universe", and yet we still believe that they have not changed at all. This is a good example of how he regarded time, space and history.

All these cannot be attributed to Buddhism or Lotus Sutra. We have to consider his geological and astronomical knowledge as well as his love of roaming and trekking in the wilderness. Even if he had assimilated the thought of the sutra by reading, it must have been difficult for him to get to that universal vision without the geological experiences he had by roaming and trekking. In this sense, he reminds us of Claude Lévi-Strauss (1908-2009) who held a similar view on space, time and history. The following quotation from *Tristes Tropiques* (1957) allows us to see the similarity of view:

> I wished a miracle to come as it does from time to time. Then it came; here and there, from hidden fissures, two green plants of different species came out side by side, each one choosing the most appropriate soil to them; and just at the same time, I could perceive in the rock two ammonites each one having different involution with high complexity indicating the gap between them of tens of thousands years. It is then that time and space suddenly fuse into one and the living diversity of the instant juxtaposes and perpetuates the ages. (Lévi-Strauss, 61)

We know that the anthropologist denounced the fallacy of the modern notion of history in quite a harsh way (Histoire et la dialectiques, in *La pensée sauvage*, 1962). Contemporary to Kenji, interested in philosophy, art and science, he opened a new perspective for the science of humans without knowing the Japanese mystic at all.

9

Kenji's best-known story for children is doubtlessly "Night on the Galactic Railroad" (Ginga Tetsudo no Yoru, 1927). This represents his cosmic view in a most comprehensive way. Based on a view inspired by Lotus Sutra, connected to the knowledge of physics, geology, biology, Kenji tried to describe the "fourth dimension" in his way. To most of us, it appears to be a fantasy, nothing more, but to him, it was a description of reality that our eyes do not see.

The main theme of the story is life and death and communication between the two. One may interpret it as communication between dream and reality, but we should bear it in mind that the author considered dream as another reality. Here is the outline of the story:

Giovanni and Campanella are classmates and good friends to each other although the one is poor and the other wealthy. On the evening of summer festival, all the classmates go to the river to celebrate Centaurus constellation, but Giovanni had to go to the milk dealer to buy some milk for his sick mother. He felt tired because after school, he worked for several hours in a print shop to earn some money, but also because he was bullied by one of his classmates because of his father who went far away without coming home.

Giovanni took a rest on a hill under the pillar called Tenki-rin, and suddenly, he found himself travelling with Campanella, his best friend, on the Galactic Railroad. The train they were on could take them anywhere at immeasurable speed all through the universe.

Campanella got off the train at Heaven Station to say farewell to Giovanni. For his mother was already there. Left alone, Giovanni continued his voyage without destination, but always in search of "real happiness".

Suddenly again, Giovanni found himself on the hill where he had been taking a rest. Remembering that he had to go for the milk for his mother, he went downtown straightaway. Coming near the river running through the town, alas, he learned that his friend Campanella was drowned to death there. Thinking of the farewell at Heaven Station, Giovanni went home with the milk for his mother. (Miyazawa, vol.10)

One of the points of the story is the coincidence of Campanella's drowning in the river with his farewell at Heaven Station. Did Kenji the author believe in what is called "synchronicity" that Wolfgang Pauli (1900-58), a quantum physicist, put forward with Karl Gustav Jung (1875-1961), a psychiatrist (Atom and Archetype: The Pauli/Jung Letters, 1932-1958) ?

One may suppose a coincidence between realty and a dream, but Giovanni and Campanella's travel on the Galactic Railroad is too coherent, too ordered, to be a dream. Kenji described it as another reality as real as our reality on earth, and he did not forget to indicate the place where the two worlds were connected: "*tenki-rin*". We are not sure of what place it is, but Kenji was.

Although they were friends connected by the soul, Kenji described Campanella and Giovanni as different souls having different aims. Both are described as searchers of real happiness, but the one is described as a pious boy who satisfied himself with being with God in Heaven while the other as an eternal searcher of the universal happiness on earth. This does not necessarily mean that the former is meant to be Christian and the latter Buddhist; Campanella may well represent Buddhism based on faith and prayer that Kenji's family held, and Giovanni the "engaged" Buddhism the author participated in. As a matter of fact, after having discovered abovementioned Lotus Sutra, he voluntarily became a member of an engaged Buddhist association, leaving his family's Buddhism based on belief in Buddha's mercy.

There are some who like to identify Kenji with Giovanni. I would rather say that Kenji was oscillating between Giovanni and Campanella. In his mind, we find a diversity of elements that contradicted one another, and he seems to have accepted all of them. Let us remember that he considered himself as an asura, the spirit split between the angelic nature and the human weakness.

10

More than once, I referred to Kenji's connection to Buddhism, more precisely to Lotus Sutra. Also did I mention his spiritualism. What was his religion then?

First, he was quite desperate about the religions of his time. As we saw earlier, he said science replaced religion without being able to offer light or warmth that religions of the past could do. This means that he felt a keen need for the renewal of religion; he wanted it to be compatible with science; he even wanted it to be scientific.

He was born to a pious family. His parents were devoted followers of *Jodo-shin* school based on absolute faith in Amitabha, the incarnation of Buddha's infinite mercy. He was raised up in that religious atmosphere.

One day, however, he happened to discover Lotus Sutra. He read it and felt a spiritual revolution bursting out within him. Since then, he abandoned his family's *Jodo-shin* school to become a follower of Lotus Sutra. He had conversion.

The difference between the two schools is fundamental. *Jodo-shin* school preaches faith and passive waiting for merciful Amitabha, the savior, while Lotus Sutra school urges its followers to act on society to make a better world. Its followers are often socially or politically militants. Kenji found it much more appropriate to his nature and the needs of his society.

Let us remember that Kenji created the school of art for the farm workers. It was to realize the ideal of Lotus Sutra. His agronomical studies aiming at improving the farm workers' material conditions also came out of the same religious conviction. Many stories he wrote for children can be considered as expressions of his faith.

His social activities coincided with the demand of a Neo-Buddhist association named *Kokuchu-kai* of which he became an active member. The association (namely, Association of National Pillars) was a newborn group of passionate Buddhists who wished Lotus Sutra to be the Bible for Japan and the Japanese. As for Neo-Buddhism, I have to say that it was a biproduct of the modernization of the whole nation. The modernizing government tried to crush Buddhism, to which Japanese Buddhists had no alternative than reforming and modernizing their religion. Abovementioned *Kokuchu-kai* was one of the outcomes of the movement.

Kenji's keen interest in science and psychology can also be considered as product of the Neo-Buddhist movement. He wanted Lotus Sutra to be more universal and more compatible with modern science.

Now, the modern government of Japan did not stop surveilling Neo-Buddhist movements, especially the one of *Kokuchu-kai* that insisted on social and political reform. Kenji's activities such as the night school for the farm workers' art became therefore an object of the local government's surveillance. Once his night school activity was publicly known, the local police summoned him to their station and interrogated him. We do not know the nature of the interrogation, but we know that he closed the school immediately after.

There is a possibility that they suspected him as a Marxist. For at that time, the government was quite afraid of Marxism spreading among the intellectuals as well as workers. They were especially cautious about the proletarian literary and artistic movements. Kenji's night school for farm workers must have been considered as one. No wonder then if the police summoned him to their station and warned him.

Besides, if he was influenced by Marxism or not, there was a revolutionary aspect in his thought. Just in the same year that he opened the night school, he wrote a story of an elephant exploited by a capitalist that ends with a kind of rebellion (Otzbel and a White Elephant, 1926). The story justifies the violence of exploited workers against a cruel exploiter. I will quote the end of the story in which the hero, a white elephant, exploited by the factory owner Otzbel, was rescued by a band of his elephant comrades that violently put an end to Otzbel's life:

Many elephants came and surrounded Otzbel's house, making the earth quake with tremendous noise. Some of them cried out "We've come to rescue you!" The imprisoned white elephant answered from the jail saying "Thanks. I am so glad that you've come!" (…) Seeing the danger falling upon him, Otzbel began to fire against them with his six-chambered revolver, but in vain. The bullets did not penetrate their thick skin. (…) It did not take long for them to break into his house. They precipitated all together inside and soon Otzbell was found completely crushed. (…) Then they rushed to the jail, broke it to get the white hero out of it. Finding him weakened and thinner than ever, they became gentle and calm and said to him "We are glad you are still alive. You are very thin though." Then they undid the heavy chain off his body to get him free. "I really appreciate your coming to save me", said the white elephant smiling sadly. (Miyazawa 10, 101-103)

The reader may wonder why the hero smiled "sadly" after having been liberated. Did he feel bad because of the violence his comrades recurred to to save him? It may be so, but we should not forget that Otzbel also used violence against them with a gun. The hero may have wished the problem to be solved peacefully, but Kenji, the author, seems to have found the use of violence unavoidable at least under certain circumstances. You may wonder how Kenji the author was not arrested for having written such a story. It is simply because he did not publish it during his lifetime.

11

I said earlier that Kenji considered psychology as the most important science and that he was much interested in psychological studies of his mind. We know that his poems were not poems to him but high-fidelity records of different states of his mind. However, the psychological states he registered do not show ordinary states of mind at all; they rather show extraordinary ones.

The reason why they are so is not difficult to find if we associate his psychological studies with William James' *The Varieties of Religious Experiences* (1902). Kenji tried to record his "religious experiences" or something relevant to them. Why did he do such enterprise? It is because he wanted to understand religious experiences in terms of psychology as James did. Besides, not only Lotus Sutra but all the teachings of Buddhism had something psychological. Buddhism started with meditations that opened the understanding of the depth of our mind. It is natural then that a modern Buddhist like Kenji tried to study psychology to update their religion.

We know that Kenji was a follower of Lotus Sutra till the end of his life. Just a few minutes before death, he is said to have said the following words to his father:

> Please make a thousand copies of Lotus Sutra translated in Japanese and give a copy to each of my friends, relatives and acquaintances. Mr. Kitamukai shall help you read proofs. I would like the following words to be written in red on the cover : "All I have done till today was for you to have this sacred book. I wish you to take the most righteous way by touching Buddha's mind through the book."
> (September 21, 1933) (Miyazawa 13, 379-380)

His father copied the words above and kept them as his will, and later, made a thousand copied of the sutra to distribute to Kenji's friends and relatives as his son wished.

With all this, one is tempted to reduce Kenji's thought to Lotus Sutra. But I would rather insist that he was not a simple follower of the sutra. Like many of Neo-Buddhists, he was oscillating between religion and science, the traditional and the modern, trying to find out the unifying point of the two. His poems and stories are crystallizations of the efforts. If we find beauty in there, it is not the beauty of the sutra but the one of the oscillations he underwent and the endeavors he made to find out the truth.

Works Cited

Dawkins, Richard: *Unweaving the Rainbow: Science, Delusion and the Appetite for Wonder*, London, Penguin Books, 2006

Jung, K.G. and Pauli, W.: *Atom and Archetype: The Pauli/Jung Letters*, 1932-1958, Princeton, Princeton University Press, 2014

Keats, John: *The Complete Poems of John Keats*, New York, Modern Library 1994

Lévi-Strauss, Claude : *Tristes Tropiques*, Paris, Plon, 1955

Lodge, Oliver: *Raymond, or Life and Death*, London, Forgotten Books, 2012

Miyazawa, Kenji: *Zen-shu* (Complete Works), Tokyo, Chikuma Publishing, 1995

Miyazawa, Kenji: Chumon no oi ryoriten, kokokubun, Japanese edition, Kindle

Penrose, Hameroff and others: *Consciousness and the Universe, Quantum Physics, Evolution, Brain and Mind*, Rawalpindi, Science Publishers, 2017

Rimbaud, Arthur: *Oeuvres*, Pocket, 1998

Ryo, Michiko: Trip to the origin of Kenji's Fourth Dimension Fantasy, 2005, on https://ryomichico.net/ sakichi/kenji-4d-timetravel.html

Weil, Simone: *La Condition Ouvrière*, Paris, Gallimard, 1951

Weil, Simone: *La pesanteur et la grâce*, Pocket, 1991